COUPLES THERAPY WORKBOOK

Strategies to Connect, Restore Love and Trust,
Improve Communication Intimacy and Validation:
A Relationship Book for Couples

A Note From The Author

I hope this book will benefit you in your journey to
increase your happiness and quality of life!

If you have not claimed your Bonus materials, do not hesitate and
get supporting materials. They will help you in your journey!

I do not spam! And only strive to provide values. For example, I only email monthly with
a free kindle book offer when amazon allows me to schedule a promotion. There are many
books in work now, and if you find the subject interesting for you, you will have a chance
to receive the kindle version free. My main interests are mental and physical health,
biohacking, and everything else that can increase happiness and quality of life. Constructive
criticism is always welcome! I am always looking for ways to improve the quality and
accessibility of the materials. Feel free to reach out to yevhenii@fiolapublishing.com.

If you find this book was helpful to you and could benefit others,
please leave a review on amazon. It would mean a word to me if you do so.

Best wishes,
Yevhenii

Table of Contents

Decoding Love:
An EFT Guide for Couples Navigating Rough Waters

The Relationship Roadmap: Three Questions to Chart Your Course

Hey there, amazing couple! We get it—navigating the rocky terrain of love isn't a cakewalk. You might feel lost, frustrated, or stuck in a rut. You're not alone. Every couple faces challenges, but knowing how to face them together is key. To do that, let's start by asking three questions that are like the North Star for your relationship:

1. **What's Going On?** - What issues are you both grappling with? This isn't about blame; it's about understanding what needs fixing.

2. **What Should Be Going On?** - What would your relationship look like if everything were hunky-dory? Imagine your 'happily ever after'—that's your goal.

3. **How Do We Get There?** - What steps can you both take to move from where you are to where you want to be?

These questions are your relationship GPS. They help you both figure out where you're stuck and how to find your way back to each other.

The Love Lens: Emotionally Focused Therapy (EFT)

You've probably heard the phrase, "Love conquers all," but let's be honest—sometimes love needs a little help. That's where Emotionally Focused Therapy (EFT) comes in. Love hasn't always gotten the attention it deserves in therapy circles. Most therapy focuses on conflict, power struggles, and individual issues, but it often overlooks the core of it all—love. It's like going to a concert and ignoring the lead singer!

EFT changes the game. It brings love back into the spotlight and offers a practical, well-researched approach to understanding what makes love tick in adult relationships. Think of it as a treasure map to unlock the secrets to a fulfilling partnership.

Why Theory Matters in Love

Okay, the word 'theory' might sound a bit academic, but trust us—having a good theory is like having a killer playlist for a road trip. It sets the mood and guides the journey. In the context of your relationship, a strong theory helps identify the root causes of your issues. It offers a roadmap for rebuilding intimacy, trust, and, yes, even love. In short, it ensures you're both focusing on what matters.

The Roots of Attachment in Adult Love

Attachment isn't just for babies and their caregivers; it's a lifelong need. Originated by John Bowlby and later applied to adult relationships, attachment theory helps explain why we act like we do in love. Are you clingy, distant, or maybe a mix of both? Understanding your attachment style can be the first step in resolving the issues that keep you both up at night.

So, as you go through this journey, remember that understanding the science of love isn't just for therapists and academics. It's for anyone who wants an emotionally fulfilling and enduring relationship. And that includes you two.

Unveiling the Secrets of Lasting Love: Understanding Attachment Theory's Ten Core Principles

1. The Lifelong Urge to Connect: Attachment as a Basic Human Need.

Hey, let's talk about the elephant in the room—dependency. Society often paints it as a weakness. Well, surprise! Attachment theory says dependency is completely natural and crucial for healthy relationships. It's not something you grow out of, like a childhood phase. The need to connect with people you care about isn't a sign of weakness; it's the "heartbeat" of any close relationship. So when you fear losing each other, know it's a universal experience. A basic part of being human makes us social creatures at our core.

2. The Balance of Independence and Dependence: Two Sides of the Same Coin.

Have you ever heard you should be "completely independent" in a relationship? Well, that's a myth. According to attachment theory, there's no such thing as complete independence or over-dependence. Instead, secure dependency and autonomy are like two peas in a pod—complementing each other. When you're securely attached, you feel more confident and independent. This sense of secure connection allows you to be authentic while still being a united couple. Research shows that secure attachment enhances your sense of self (Mikulincer, 1995). In other words, belonging to someone helps you become who you're meant to be.

3. Your Safe Haven: The Comfort of Attachment.

We all have moments when life gets overwhelming. When that happens, being close to someone you love feels like fresh air. That's not just poetic language; it's backed by science. Your loved one's proximity has a calming effect on your nervous system (Schore, 1994). Think of your relationship as a safe haven that shields you from life's stress and uncertainties. This emotional comfort zone is essential for your ongoing personal growth and mental well-being.

4. The Launching Pad: Secure Attachment as Your Basecamp for Exploration.

Imagine your relationship as a secure base, like the home base in a game of tag. This safe place allows you to explore the world, take risks, and be open to new experiences. A secure attachment makes you feel safe and empowers you to be adventurous and open to life's possibilities. This "home base" in your relationship enriches your ability to reflect on yourself and adapt to new challenges (Mikulincer, 1997). It's like having a co-pilot in the journey of life.

5. The Building Blocks: Emotional Accessibility and Responsiveness.

Let's be real—physical presence isn't enough. You could be sitting next to each other and yet feel worlds apart. Emotional engagement is the magic ingredient that builds and sustains a secure bond. When you're emotionally accessible and responsive to each other, you're telling your partner, "You matter to me." On the flip side, a lack of emotional responsiveness sends a message that can be devastating: "You don't matter, and we're not connected." Emotions are attachment language; they communicate your deepest needs and desires. They're the rhythm to your relationship's melody.

6. Weathering Life's Storms: Attachment Needs in Tough Times.

Life can throw curveballs, whether a stressful job, illness, or even a seemingly harmless flirtation at a party. During these times, your attachment needs for comfort and connection amplify. Think of your attachment to each other as your emotional safety net. It helps you bounce back when life tries to knock you down. So, it's natural to seek each other out when feeling vulnerable. Remember, the need for a loving connection isn't a weakness; it's your built-in mechanism for coping with life's challenges.

7. The Emotional Rollercoaster: The Phases of Separation Distress.

Feeling ignored or neglected? You're likely to go through a cycle of emotions: first anger, then clinginess, followed by depression, and eventually, detachment. Attachment theory explains these reactions as completely normal responses to feeling disconnected. So, when you find yourselves locked in a pattern of demand and withdrawal, understand it's often a cry for emotional connection. Recognizing these patterns as calls for closeness can be the first step in breaking the cycle and finding your way back to each other.

8. Coping Styles: The Limited Ways We Deal With Emotional Distance.

Have you ever wondered why some people appear clingy while others seem aloof? Attachment theory identifies two main coping strategies when emotional needs aren't met—becoming anxious and clingy or avoiding emotional engagement altogether. Both strategies can become habits that dictate how you interact with each other, often worsening your relationship woes. Recognizing these coping styles can help you understand what you're fighting about and how to break the cycle.

9. The Stories We Tell Ourselves: Working Models of Self and Other.

Each of you carries a mental script shaped by past experiences, which influences how you view yourselves and each other. These "working models" can guide your actions and reactions in your relationship. For example, if you're securely attached, you likely view yourself as lovable and your partner as reliable. But you may doubt your worth and your partner's commitment if you're insecurely attached. Understanding these narratives can reveal the emotional truths that bubble up during heated moments, helping you rewrite the script for a healthier relationship.

10. The Profound Impact of Isolation and Loss: Attachment as a Theory of Trauma.

Attachment theory is, at its heart, a theory of trauma. It recognizes that feelings of isolation and loss are deeply traumatizing. The emotional security that comes from knowing your partner will be there for you affects your relationship and impacts your well-being. Confidence in each other's reliability can be a buffer against the chronic fears and stresses that life throws your way.

Attachment theory is more than academic jargon; it's a lens through which to understand the intricate dance of love and emotional connection. Whether you find yourself stuck in a cycle of demand and withdrawal or coping with emotional distance, the principles of attachment theory can guide you toward a deeper, more satisfying relationship. So, are you ready to explore these ideas and put them into practice? Because understanding your emotional self can be the key to unlocking a love that lasts.

The Lifelong Dance of Attachment: What Every Couple Should Know

The Universality of Attachment Needs: From Childhood to Adulthood.

You've probably heard the saying, "Love makes the world go 'round," but have you ever considered why that is? It's all about attachment—a universal need, not just for kids. Both children and adults crave attention, emotional responsiveness, and a deep connection with their loved ones. Whether you're five or fifty, the presence of a trusted person makes life's challenges more bearable and even boosts your ability to handle stress. What's more, when your partner is emotionally available and responsive, you're not just happier—you're also better at navigating the ups and downs of your relationship.

The Transformative Power of Emotional Presence

You might become anxious and preoccupied if your partner is distant or unresponsive. Just like a child feels safer when their caregiver is near, adults, too, need that emotional security to engage with the world around them fully. This emotional rope isn't just about physical presence but also nonverbal cues. From the way you look at each other to the tender moments of physical touch like hugging or kissing, emotional presence is the glue that binds your relationship.

The Safe Haven: Your Emotional Anchor in Life's Storms

Separation from a loved one—whether it's physical or emotional—triggers distress at any age. It's why you both rejoice at each other's company, especially if you've been apart. It's why you share experiences, confide secrets, and even find yourselves thinking about how the other would react to certain events. This emotional sanctuary is what everyone seeks, from the time they're in the crib to their final days.

The Unique Characteristics of Adult Attachments

However, adult relationships do differ from parent-child bonds in a few key ways:

1. **Mental Comfort:** As adults, you can find solace in your mental representation of your partner, even when apart. Unlike children, who may need physical presence for comfort, adults can carry the image of their loved ones in their minds as a source of emotional security.

2. **The Role of Sexuality**: Sex isn't just about physical pleasure or procreation; it's an attachment behavior. Ever wonder why intimacy feels so emotionally satisfying? It's because oxytocin, often called the "cuddle hormone," is released during sexual climax. Interestingly, activities that are deeply bonding in nature, like kissing, are often avoided in situations where sex is purely transactional.

3. **Reciprocity:** While a parent-child relationship is more one-sided, with the parent providing the most emotional support, adult relationships thrive on mutual give-and-take. Each partner contributes to the emotional well-being of the relationship, making it a two-way street.

So, why is this all important? Understanding the underlying principles of attachment can offer you a roadmap for navigating the complexities of your relationship. Knowing that your attachment needs are normal can free you both to seek out the emotional connection that makes life richer and more fulfilling. After all, from the cradle to the grave, we all want someone to hold us in the dark.

The Evolution of Attachment in Adult Relationships: The Timeline and Its Implications

The Maturation of Adult Bonds: Beyond Friendship.

While the flicker of friendship may ignite the spark in a new relationship, it's often not until about two years in that the attachment flame truly starts to burn. This timeline isn't arbitrary; it suggests that your shared emotional bonds need time to mature and deepen. So, if you're in the early stages of your relationship and you're not feeling that soul-stirring attachment just yet, don't worry—you're likely still in the "stimulation mode" of friendship.

Reacting to Emotional Distance: More Than Just "Communication Issues"

Have you ever noticed how even a short emotional distance can send you both into a tailspin? That's not just a "communication problem" or a temporary hiccup in your closeness. It's your inbuilt, adaptive response to the perceived loss of your primary emotional and physical security source. So, the next time you feel like the other is "overreacting," it might be helpful to remember that this is a natural reaction to losing your emotional anchor.

Rethinking Relationship Distress: It's Not Just About Conflict

Contrary to popular belief, marital distress or the risk of divorce doesn't primarily come from negative emotions, conflicts, or bad interactions. While those factors may be the visible signs, the root often lies in the absence of emotionally responsive interactions. The real trouble begins when you or your partner fail to meet each other's attachment needs. The emotional distance and deprivation trigger conflicts and unhappiness, not vice versa.

The Healing Power of Secure Attachment: Ending Long-Standing Arguments

The good news is that once you start responding to each other's emotional needs and cues, your bond strengthens. With a secure attachment as your base, you'll find that many of your long-standing disagreements resolve themselves naturally. And even when arguments do arise, they won't have the power to shake the foundations of your relationship.

So, it's not just about avoiding conflicts or working on communication skills—though those are important. At the core, it's about understanding and meeting each other's emotional and attachment needs. When you both get this right, it becomes the game-changer that can turn a troubled relationship into a fulfilling and resilient partnership.

Attachment Theory as the Compass for Couple Therapy

The Multifaceted Nature of Attachment Theory

At its core, attachment theory serves as an integrative framework for couple therapy. It combines behavioral, systemic, and emotional lenses to examine the complexities of relationships. Whether looking at it from an evolutionary standpoint or as an individual dynamic, the theory combines multiple perspectives to explain how and why we connect with our partners or fail to connect.

The Constant Dance: Attachment in Everyday Interactions

In relationships, attachment isn't just an internal mindset; it's a continual dance between partners. Your attachment style doesn't just reside within you; it's reflected, influenced, and even reshaped in your interactions with your loved one. This means that attachment styles can change as you learn and grow within your relationship. And that's good news for any couple looking to improve their connection.

The Nuts and Bolts: From Emotional Reactivity to Communication Competence

Understanding attachment styles can help you make sense of your emotional triggers and reactions. It explains why one of you might become anxious and needy when the other starts pulling away. But more than just offering insights, it provides a roadmap for change. For example, secure attachment promotes effective communication and collaborative problem-solving. So, focusing on building a secure attachment can be the first step toward breaking free from destructive cycles like 'demand–withdraw.'

The Bigger Picture: Attachment Theory as a Unifying Force

As couple therapy evolves, there's a convergence between theory, research, and practice, and attachment theory is at the heart. It offers a comprehensive approach integrating emotional dynamics, specific interactional patterns, and attachment security. Ultimately, it provides a unified direction for couple therapy, highlighting that fostering secure attachment bonds is the key to resolving relationship distress.

So, if you're grappling with relationship difficulties, remember that attachment theory isn't just academic jargon. It's a practical, evidence-based guide that can help you understand the 'why' behind your relationship challenges and offers actionable steps to foster a secure, loving relationship.

The Transformative Power of Attachment Theory in Couple Therapy

Key Benefits of Using Attachment Theory in Couple Therapy

1. Clear Conceptualization: Attachment theory provides a clear framework to understand the health and dysfunction in relationships. It offers specific goals and endpoints for therapy, such as fostering a secure bond between partners.

2. Depathologizing Perspective: It reframes the emotional distress and reactions in a relationship in a way that fosters understanding and compassion rather than judgment and alienation. This can make the therapy session a haven.

3. Focused Intervention: The theory helps zero in on the core issues like attachment emotions, fears, longings, and patterns of interaction. This enables getting lost in the drama and content issues, making the therapeutic process more effective.

4. Sustainable Change: Attachment theory helps structure new enduring emotional experiences because they resonate with our basic neurobiology. This has the added advantage of preventing relapse, a common issue with other therapeutic models.

The Attachment Inventory: A Detailed How-To Manual

Objective

This exercise aims to help couples understand their individual attachment styles. By identifying these styles, couples can better understand their emotional triggers, needs, and how they relate to each other. This exercise lays the groundwork for deepening emotional bonds and fostering a secure relationship.

Materials Needed

Attachment Style Questionnaire for each partner (can be found in various psychology and relationship books or online resources)

Pen or pencil

Quiet space to discuss

Duration

Approximately 30-45 minutes

Preparation:

- Sit down in a quiet space where you can focus without distractions.
- Have the Attachment Style Questionnaires and pens/pencils ready.

Individual Assessment:

- Each partner takes 10-15 minutes to complete the Attachment Style Questionnaire.

Review Your Answers:

- Once you've both finished, review your results to understand your predominant attachment style (Secure, Anxious, Avoidant, or Fearful-Avoidant).

Share and Discuss

- Take turns sharing your predominant attachment style and the traits or behaviors that accurately describe you.
- Discuss how you see these traits manifesting in your relationship.

Explore Real-world Instances:

- Share specific instances where you felt your attachment style was evident in your relationship. You could feel particularly secure, anxious, or avoidant in this situation.

Discuss Emotional Triggers and Needs:

- Discuss the emotional triggers or situations that make you feel insecure or anxious in the relationship.
- Discuss the emotional needs that, when met, make you feel secure and loved.

Reflect on Partner's Style:

- Reflect on how your partner's attachment style complements or conflicts with your own. Discuss ways you can be more attuned to each other's attachment needs.

Create Action Points:

- Based on your discussion, create a few action points or commitments to help each other meet attachment needs. For example, if one partner has an anxious attachment style, an action point could be to offer more verbal affirmations of love and commitment.

Benefits

Provides a structured framework to understand each partner's emotional landscape.
Opens up dialogue about often overlooked emotional needs and fears.
Creates actionable insights into how to provide emotional support to each other.

Tips for Success

Be honest in your responses; the exercise only works if you're honest and open.

This is not a blame game. The idea is to understand, not to criticize or stigmatize each other.

If discussions get heated, take a break and return to the conversation when both of you are calm.

Attachment Style Questionnaire for Couples

This questionnaire will help you identify your predominant attachment style: Secure, Anxious, Avoidant, or Fearful-Avoidant. Answer each question honestly, thinking about how you generally feel in close relationships, especially romantic ones.

Instructions

For each statement below, rate how well it describes you on a scale of 1 to 5, where:

1 = Strongly Disagree

2 = Disagree

3 = Neutral

4 = Agree

5 = Strongly Agree

Questionnaire

1. I find it relatively easy to get close to others.

   ▸

   ▸

   ▸

   ▸

   ▸

2. I often worry that my partner doesn't really love me.

   ▸

   ▸

   ▸

   ▸

   ▸

3. I prefer not to show a partner how I feel deep down.

   ▸

   ▸

   ▸

   ▸

   ▸

4. I feel comfortable depending on others.

   ▸

   ▸

   ▸

   ▸

   ▸

5. I often worry that my partner will abandon me.

   ▸

   ▸

   ▸

   ▸

   ▸

6. I find it difficult to trust people completely.

   ▸

   ▸

   ▸

   ▸

   ▸

7. I'm comfortable with my partner depending on me.

   ▸

   ▸

   ▸

   ▸

   ▸

8. I worry about being alone.

   -
   -
   -
   -
   -

9. I feel uneasy opening up to others.

   -
   -
   -
   -
   -

10. I feel secure in my relationships.

   -
   -
   -
   -
   -

Scoring

Secure Attachment: High scores on questions 1, 4, 7, and 10.

Anxious Attachment: High scores on questions 2, 5, and 8.

Avoidant Attachment: High scores on questions 3, 6, and 9.

Add up the scores for each set of questions corresponding to an attachment style. The highest total score indicates your predominant attachment style.

Interpretation

Secure Attachment: You feel comfortable with intimacy and are usually warm and loving.

Anxious Attachment: You crave intimacy, are often preoccupied with your relationships, and worry about your partner's ability to love you.

Avoidant Attachment: You equate intimacy with losing independence and constantly try to minimize closeness.

Please note that this is a simplified self-assessment tool and not a substitute for professional advice. If you find that attachment issues are causing significant problems in your relationship, it may be helpful to consult a trained therapist.

WEEK 1

Communication

The Foundations of Communication

The ABCs of Communication

Communication is often compared to a complex dance where both parties continuously adjust their steps to remain in sync. However, we must understand the basic steps before diving into intricate dance moves. So, what are the fundamental elements of communication? Let's start with the basics—verbal and non-verbal cues and the art of active listening.

Verbal and Non-Verbal: Two Sides of the Same Coin

Words are powerful, indeed, but they're not the whole story. While verbal communication is explicit, non-verbal cues often fill in the gaps and provide context. Imagine you're telling your partner about your rough day at work, and they respond with a simple 'uh-huh' while scrolling through their phone. That one dismissive gesture can speak louder than a thousand words, signaling a lack of interest or empathy.

On the flip side, a warm hug or a gentle touch can convey support and love more effectively than mere words. Non-verbal cues like eye contact, facial expressions, and body language are the unsung heroes that add depth and dimension to our conversations. They can affirm, negate, or even contradict the spoken word, making them an essential aspect of effective communication.

Active Listening: The Unsung Hero

Now, let's discuss a crucial but often overlooked element—active listening. Listening is more than passive; it's an active process of hearing, understanding, interpreting, and evaluating what is being said. It's like tuning into a radio frequency so clear that you can hear the lyrics and catch the emotion in the singer's voice.

Active listening involves giving full attention to the speaker and showing your involvement through small verbal or non-verbal cues like nodding, making eye contact, or simply saying, 'I understand.' By actively listening, you're making the speaker feel valued and gaining a more profound understanding of the discussion.

The Symphony of Verbal and Non-Verbal Communication with Active Listening

So, how do these elements come together? Think of it as a symphony where each instrument has its unique sound but collectively produces a harmonious melody. Verbal communication is your lead violin, setting the tone and direction. Non-verbal cues are the supporting instruments that enrich the composition, while active listening is the conductor, orchestrating the flow and ensuring every note is heard and understood.

In the realm of relationships, mastering the synergy between verbal and non-verbal communication, coupled with active listening, can turn ordinary conversations into meaningful dialogue. It's about striking the right balance, knowing when to speak, when to listen, and when to let your body do the talking.

Barriers to Effective Communication

Identifying and Understanding Common Barriers to Effective Communication

Communication isn't always smooth sailing; sometimes, we hit choppy waters. These choppy waters are often the barriers that impede open and effective dialogue between partners. By understanding these barriers, you can learn to navigate around them or, better yet, remove them altogether.

The Silent Treatment

Ah, the infamous silent treatment, where silence isn't golden but a shade of icy blue. This form of emotional stonewalling serves as a barrier by shutting down any form of constructive conversation, leaving the other person in a guessing game of 'what did I do wrong?'

Insulting Remarks and Hurtful Language

Insults and derogatory language are the antithesis of healthy communication. They don't just injure the recipient emotionally but also sever the threads of mutual respect that are vital for any meaningful interaction.

Screaming and Yelling

Raising the volume doesn't amplify the validity of your point. Screaming and yelling often cloud the issue, turning a potentially productive conversation into a vocal competition.

Not Communicating What You Need

Sometimes, the barrier is what's not said. Failing to articulate your needs and expectations leaves your partner in the dark, making it impossible for them to meet you halfway.

Half-Listening

Listening with one ear and planning your next retort with the other? That's half-listening. This approach turns communication into a debate rather than a dialogue, where the goal is to win rather than understand.

Wrong Timing

Timing is everything, even in communication. Picking the wrong moment to discuss important issues can be counterproductive, as the other person may not be emotionally or mentally prepared for the conversation.

Assumptions and Criticisms

Assumptions are the termites of communication. They slowly eat away at the foundation, creating misunderstandings and misconceptions. Coupled with criticisms, they can make any dialogue counterproductive.

Gaslighting

Gaslighting is a manipulative tactic where one person tries to make the other doubt their reality or judgment. It's a toxic barrier that erodes trust and makes open communication almost impossible.

Effects of Poor Communication

Exploring the Consequences of Poor Communication in Relationships

It's easy to underestimate the power of a simple conversation—or the lack thereof. Poor communication doesn't just lead to awkward silences or heated arguments; it can have lasting effects that ripple through your relationship, affecting both emotional and mental well-being.

Depression

When communication breaks down, feelings of loneliness and disconnection can quickly set in, often leading to depression. The absence of open dialogue creates a void, leaving individuals feeling unsupported and misunderstood.

Anxiety

Poor communication can also breed anxiety. The unpredictability of not knowing what your partner is thinking or feeling can create tension and worry.

Antagonism

The erosion of effective communication can cultivate antagonism between partners. When conversations turn into battlegrounds, a sense of animosity takes root, making it challenging to resolve conflicts amicably.

Disconnection

One of the most apparent effects of poor communication is emotional disconnection. When you can't effectively communicate your thoughts, feelings, and needs, an emotional gap widens between you and your partner, leading to a loss of intimacy and connection.

Toxic Relationship

Continual miscommunication can escalate into a toxic relationship. The lack of clarity, understanding, and respect makes the relationship unsustainable in the long term, causing more harm than good to both parties.

Resentment

When issues are left unspoken or unresolved due to poor communication, resentment can build up over time. This emotional baggage becomes a barrier, making future communication even more challenging.

Emotional Isolation

Ultimately, the endgame of poor communication is emotional isolation. When dialogue breaks down completely, individuals often retreat into their emotional shells, isolating themselves to avoid further hurt or misunderstanding.

Communication Styles

Understanding Different Communication Styles and Their Impact

Just as people have unique fingerprints, they also have distinct communication styles. These styles not only define how you express yourself but also influence the dynamics of your relationship. Knowing these styles can help you adapt your communication strategies for more meaningful interactions.

Passive

The passive communicator often avoids confrontation and may not speak up when they should. While this approach may avoid immediate conflict, it can lead to resentment and a lack of genuine connection in the relationship.

Aggressive

The aggressive communicator has no problem making their thoughts and feelings known but often at the expense of others. This style may get the point across but can also cause emotional harm and create a hostile environment.

Passive-Aggressive

A passive-aggressive communicator may not openly express their feelings but will make them known through indirect actions or comments. This style is confusing and can lead to misunderstandings and resentment over time.

Assertive

The assertive communicator can express their thoughts and feelings clearly without hurting others. This is often considered the most effective communication style, encouraging open dialogue and mutual respect.

Manipulative

Manipulative communicators use conversation as a tool to control or influence others. This style undermines trust and can have detrimental effects on the relationship.

Open/Direct

Open or direct communicators value honesty and clarity. They speak their minds clearly and listen well to their partners. This style encourages healthy communication but requires both parties to be receptive and respectful.

Improve Your Communication Skills

Improving communication isn't just about talking more; it's about talking better. And better communication involves a full spectrum of skills, from active listening to emotional regulation. Whether you're an eloquent speaker or tend to fumble over your words, there's always room for improvement. This chapter offers strategies to communicate and connect meaningfully with your partner.

Active Listening Techniques

Active listening is not just a skill; it's an art form. It involves hearing your partner's words and truly understanding their emotions and intentions. Techniques like 'reflective listening' can be invaluable here. This involves repeating what you heard to ensure you've captured both the content and the feeling behind what was said. Another technique is 'paraphrasing,' where you restate your partner's point in your own words, clarifying misunderstandings immediately.

Active Listening Strategies

Beyond the techniques are the strategies that make active listening a habit. One such strategy is to 'listen first, react later.' Instead of mentally preparing your rebuttal while your partner is still talking, focus solely on their words and let your responses come naturally afterward. 'Empathetic listening' is another strategy where you put yourself in your partner's shoes, trying to understand their perspective before offering your own.

Body Language Awareness

Communication isn't just verbal; your body speaks volumes too. Being aware of your body language, as well as your partner's, can enrich your conversations. A simple nod can affirm that you're engaged, while eye contact can foster a deeper emotional connection. Conversely, crossed arms might signal defensiveness, and lack of eye contact could indicate discomfort or dishonesty.

Emotion Regulation Techniques

Let's face it: conversations can get heated. That's where emotion regulation techniques come in. Techniques like 'deep breathing' or 'counting to ten' can help you maintain your composure. Understanding your 'emotional triggers' can also be enlightening, helping you navigate conversations without becoming confrontations.

Questioning Techniques

Asking questions is a powerful tool for effective communication. But not all questions are created equal. 'Open-ended questions' invite your partner to share more, turning a monologue into a dialogue. 'Clarifying questions' can help resolve ambiguities, ensuring you and your partner are on the same page. Questioning also involves knowing when not to question; sometimes, a supportive statement or a compassionate silence can be more impactful.

Emotional Triggers

Emotional triggers can often be likened to invisible tripwires in the intricate maze of human relationships. These triggers are deeply rooted in personal experiences, psychological make-up, and sometimes even hidden fears or insecurities. They can turn a casual conversation into a full-blown emotional conflict when activated. Recognizing and understanding these triggers is a crucial first step toward navigating the complex emotional terrains of interpersonal relationships, particularly with intimate partners.

Examples of Emotional Triggers

The landscape of emotional triggers is vast, complex, and highly individualized. However, certain triggers tend to be universal due to shared human experiences and psychological tendencies. Let's delve deeper into some of these commonly experienced emotional triggers:

Criticism: The experience of being criticized often strikes at the core of individual self-esteem. Whether it's constructive or destructive, criticism can evoke strong emotional reactions. It can make people defensive and less receptive, closing the door on effective, meaningful communication.

Rejection: The fear or experience of rejection cuts deep. It can trigger primal fears of abandonment, leading to a wide range of reactive behaviors— from emotional withdrawal to overt aggression. This trigger can make rational conversation difficult, if not impossible.

Feeling Unheard: The sensation of talking without being heard can be deeply invalidating. It can ignite feelings of marginalization and unimportance, leading to resentment or overt confrontations as individuals 'fight' to be heard.

Loss of Control: For some people, control equates to stability. The mere perception of losing control can trigger anxiety, aggressive behavior, or emotional shutdown. This can make balanced, equitable communication a significant challenge.

Betrayal: Real or perceived acts of betrayal can trigger a volcano of emotions, from anger and hurt to despair. This emotional upheaval often makes calm, reasoned discussion extremely challenging, leading to retaliatory actions or complete withdrawal.

Injustice: Feeling unfairly treated can trigger powerful emotions like indignation, anger, or resentment. These emotions can cloud rational judgment, leading to confrontational or defensive communication styles.

Jealousy: Jealousy is a complex emotional cocktail of insecurity, fear, and envy. When triggered, it can cloud rational judgment and lead to accusatory or passive-aggressive communication styles.

Abandonment: The fear of abandonment is often rooted in past experiences and can trigger a wide range of emotional responses, from heightened emotional clinging to pre-emptive emotional or physical distancing.

Failure: The fear or reality of failure can be a significant trigger, stirring up feelings of inadequacy, shame, or defensiveness. These emotions can make open and honest communication difficult.

Identity Challenges: Challenges to one's core beliefs, values, or self-perception can be extremely triggering. Questions or statements that shake the foundation of an individual's self-identity can evoke strong emotional responses, often leading to defensive or aggressive communication.

The Role of Apology and Forgiveness

In the intricate dance of human relationships, apology and forgiveness bring grace to your movements. They're the harmonizers that tune a discordant interaction into a harmonious conversation. But these aren't just words or actions; they're complex emotional processes that require self-awareness, humility, and a deep understanding of human frailty. Mastering the art of sincere apology and genuine forgiveness is not just a social grace but a relationship lifesaver.

The Anatomy of a Genuine Apology

An apology isn't just saying, 'I'm sorry.' It's a multi-layered emotional and intellectual acknowledgment of wrongdoing. A genuine apology has several key components:

Acknowledgment of Wrongdoing: The first step is acknowledging what you did wrong without any 'buts' or conditions. It shows you understand the impact of your actions.

Understanding the Impact: A real apology goes beyond acknowledgment and extends into understanding your actions' emotional, psychological, or even physical impact on the other person.

Expressing Regret: This is the emotional core of the apology. It's where you express genuine sorrow or regret for your actions without making it about your guilt or shame.

Commitment to Change: An apology is empty without a commitment to avoid repeating the wrongdoing. This shows you're serious about making amends.

The Power of Forgiveness

Forgiveness is not a sign of weakness; it's a sign of emotional intelligence and strength. It doesn't mean forgetting or condoning the wrongdoing but releasing the emotional burden of holding a grudge. Forgiveness is a gift you give not just to your partner but also to yourself.

Emotional Liberation: Holding onto grudges or resentment is emotionally taxing. Forgiveness allows you to free yourself from the emotional shackles of past wrongs.

Fostering Emotional Safety: Mutual forgiveness creates an environment of emotional safety where both partners feel secure enough to be vulnerable, enhancing the quality of communication.

Building Resilience in Relationships: Forgiveness adds a layer of resilience to relationships. An emotional cushion helps you bounce back from the inevitable bumps and jolts of interpersonal interactions.

The Dance of Apology and Forgiveness

Apology and forgiveness are most effective when they work in tandem. An apology opens the door to reconciliation, and forgiveness seals it with emotional integrity. Together, they form a powerful duo that can mend broken communication lines, heal emotional wounds, and fortify the foundations of a loving relationship.

Psychological Biases in Communication

If communication is an art, then psychological biases are unintentional brush strokes that can either add unexpected beauty or ruin the masterpiece. These biases often operate under the radar, subtly influencing how we perceive, interpret, and react during conversations. Uncovering these hidden drivers of communication is not just an intellectual exercise; it's a journey toward more authentic and effective interpersonal interactions.

Confirmation Bias

Imagine you're wearing tinted glasses that only allow you to see what you already believe. That's confirmation bias for you. It's the tendency to search for, interpret, or remember information in a way that confirms your preconceptions. In conversations, this means you're more likely to disregard what doesn't fit into your existing belief system, leading to skewed communication.

Fundamental Attribution Error

This is the bias where you attribute someone else's behavior to their character rather than situational factors. If your partner forgets to take out the trash, you might think they're lazy or uncaring, overlooking possible external reasons like stress or forgetfulness. This bias can turn molehills into mountains in relationships, making it difficult to resolve issues constructively.

Anchoring Bias

The anchoring bias is when you rely too heavily on the first piece of information you receive. If your partner comes home grumpy, you might anchor to that mood as a reflection of their feelings towards you, neglecting any subsequent signs that suggest otherwise. This can lead to unnecessary emotional turmoil and misunderstandings.

Self-Serving Bias

In this bias, individuals attribute positive events to their character but negative events to external factors. In a relationship, this means taking credit for what goes well but blaming your partner or circumstances for what goes wrong. This can create an imbalance in the relationship, breeding resentment and hindering open communication.

Halo Effect

This is the tendency to let one positive quality of a person overshadow other, more negative qualities. If your partner is exceptionally kind, you might overlook other less favorable behaviors, leading to a skewed perception that can cloud judgment and communication.

Negativity Bias

This is the tendency to give more weight to negative experiences over neutral or positive experiences. A single negative comment can overshadow an entire day of positive interaction. Recognizing this bias can help you balance your emotional reactions and contribute to healthier communication dynamics.

The Role of Biases in Communication

Understanding these biases doesn't just make you 'bias-aware'; it makes you 'communication-aware.' Recognizing how these cognitive shortcuts affect your interactions can be an eye-opener, leading to more deliberate, thoughtful, and effective communication. It's like cleaning the lens through which you view your relationship, allowing for a clearer, more accurate picture.

Conclusion

If relationships are an ongoing journey, this workbook has been your travel guide, a compass for navigating the complex terrains of communication. As you close this book, remember that the journey doesn't end here; it merely takes a new turn, equipped with a toolbox of strategies, techniques, and a renewed sense of self-awareness.

We've explored various topics, from verbal and non-verbal communication to the intricacies of emotional triggers and psychological biases. We've delved into the roles of apology and forgiveness and even ventured into the digital world to examine how technology impacts our relationships. Each chapter has equipped you with actionable tips and exercises to bring these concepts to life.

The journey ahead is filled with both challenges and opportunities. The key is to apply what you've learned here in a way that resonates with your unique relationship dynamics. There's no one-size-fits-all approach to communication, but the strategies and insights you've gained will serve as guiding lights.

Your Personalized Workbook

While this workbook offers a structured approach, it's designed to be flexible. The exercises provided don't have to be taken in the order they are listed. Feel free to pick and choose exercises that resonate with you and are most appropriate for the specific challenges or circumstances you're facing. Consider this workbook as a menu of options, not a set sequence of steps.

Chapter Exercises

Exercise: The 'I Feel' Statements: Speaking Your Truth Without Throwing Shade

Introduction

Ah, the classic 'You always' or 'You never' statements—nothing spices up an argument like some good ol' blame seasoning, right? Well, not quite. It's time to switch things up and drop the 'you' like it's hot. Welcome to 'I Feel' Statements, where we focus on expressing ourselves without putting our partners on the defensive. You'll learn to communicate your feelings and needs without making it sound like a courtroom indictment.

Objective

If you accept it, your mission is to shift from blaming and accusatory language to a more empathetic and understanding form of communication. By using 'I feel' statements, you'll not only make your conversations more civil but also deepen the emotional connection with your partner.

Duration

This exercise can be done in one session of about 30-40 minutes or spread over a week with smaller, bite-sized conversations. And no, you don't get to say, 'I feel like you should do this faster.' Nice try, though.

Materials Needed

- A quiet, comfortable space free from distractions
- A genuine willingness to communicate (no eye-rolling allowed!)
- Pen and paper for optional note-taking

Instructions

1. **Set the Stage**: Find a quiet and comfortable space to talk without distractions. Yes, that means putting the phones down—don't worry, Instagram will still be there when you're done.

2. **Identify the Topic**: Choose a topic or issue you've recently argued about or been swept under the rug. No, deciding what to have for dinner doesn't count unless it somehow led to World War III in your household.

3. **Construct Your Statements**: Take turns crafting 'I feel' statements related to the chosen topic. For example, instead of saying, 'You never listen to me,' try, 'I feel unheard when you're on your phone during our conversations.'

4. **Active Listening**: When one partner shares, the other's job is to listen—really listen. Avoid planning your courtroom rebuttal. Your partner should mirror what they heard to ensure they got it right.

5. **Empathetic Response**: The listener should empathetically validate the speaker's feelings, like 'I can see why you would feel that way.' No sarcastic 'Well, I feel like you're overreacting' allowed.

6. **Switch Roles**: Once the first partner has expressed their 'I feel' statement and received validation, switch roles and repeat the process.

Points for Reflection

- How did the dynamics of the conversation change when using 'I feel' statements?
- Was it challenging to express your feelings without blaming your partner?
- Did the empathetic responses from your partner make you feel more understood and less defensive?

Tips for Success

- The objective is not to solve all your problems in one go but to communicate more effectively.
- Keep practicing. This is like emotional Pilates—the more you do it, the more flexible your communication muscles will become.

Closing Thoughts

Remember, communication in a relationship is not about winning an argument but understanding each other. Using 'I feel' statements is a step towards creating a safe emotional space for you and your partner. So, go ahead and feel your feelings—make sure you express them in a way that invites conversation, not confrontation.

Exercise: Nonverbal Communication Game-Let's Face It, Words Are Overrated

Introduction

Who needs words when you've got eyebrows that can practically speak Latin? Welcome to the Nonverbal Communication Game, where your face and body do the talking. Discover how much you can convey—and how much you can understand—without uttering a single word.

Objective

This exercise aims to explore the power of nonverbal cues in communication. Learn to read and emit signals through facial expressions, gestures, and body language.

Duration

This is a quick and fun exercise, ideally done in a 15-20 minute session. Perfect for those moments when you're both tired of talking but still want to connect.

Materials Needed

- A comfortable, well-lit room (it's tough to read facial expressions in the dark)
- Open-mindedness and a sense of humor (mandatory)

Instructions

1. **Warm-Up:** Start by sitting facing each other. Take a deep breath to center yourselves. No peeking at your phones!
2. **Round 1 - Charades Style:** One partner will communicate a simple emotion or action without using words. There are no sounds, just facial expressions and gestures.
3. **Guess:** The other partner tries to guess what emotion or action was communicated. No pressure, it's not 'Who Wants to Be a Millionaire?'.
4. **Round 2 - Mimicry:** One partner makes a facial expression, and the other tries to mimic it as closely as possible.
5. **Switch Roles:** After each round, switch roles and repeat.
6. **Feedback:** Share your experience. Was it harder or easier than you thought?

Points for Reflection
- What surprised you about this exercise?
- Did you discover any 'go-to' gestures or expressions you weren't aware of?
- How well did you think you understood your partner, and vice versa?

Tips for Success
- Don't overthink it. The point is to be as natural as possible.
- Feel free to be dramatic; sometimes, exaggeration makes understanding easier.
- Keep the energy light and fun. This is not the time for your best De Niro impression (unless it makes you both laugh).

Closing Thoughts
Whether you discovered you're a natural mime or that you could use a little work on your nonverbal cues, the point is to learn and grow. So the next time you're at a loss for words, just remember: Your face and body have a language all their own. Learn it, and you'll add a whole new layer to your communication skills.

Exercise: Role Reversal-Walk a Mile in My Emotional Shoes

Introduction
Ever wondered what it's like to be on the other side of an argument with you? Well, now's your chance to find out! Welcome to 'Role Reversal,' an exercise that allows you to switch roles with your partner during a hypothetical conflict. It's like acting in a drama, but the script is your life.

Objective
This exercise aims to understand how your partner experiences conflict and validation in your relationship. By stepping into their shoes, you can better understand their emotional landscape.

Duration

Allocate 20-30 minutes for this exercise. It's a small time investment for a potentially eye-opening experience.

Materials Needed

- A quiet and comfortable space free of distractions
- A topic or past argument that both partners agree is worth exploring
- A willingness to be vulnerable and open-minded

Instructions

1. **Choose a Topic**: Agree on a past argument or issue that you're both comfortable revisiting.
2. **Set Boundaries**: Make it clear that this is a role-reversal exercise meant for understanding, not mocking or criticizing.
3. **Switch Roles**: Each partner assumes the other's role in the chosen argument. Try to mimic the words, tone, and body language.
4. **Act It Out**: Have the 'argument' while role-reversed. Remember, you're playing the other person.
5. **Reflect**: After the role-reversal, return to your roles and discuss what you learned or felt.

Points for Reflection

- How did it feel to argue from your partner's perspective?
- Were there any 'Aha!' moments where you understood why your partner reacts a certain way?
- Did the exercise change how you view validation in your relationship?

Tips for Success

- Keep it respectful. This is an exercise in empathy, not a chance to caricature your partner.
- Be as honest as possible in your reflections. The value of this exercise lies in its ability to uncover hidden insights.
- If the exercise triggers strong emotions, pausing and processing before discussing is okay.

Closing Thoughts

'Role Reversal' is like a mirror that allows you to see yourself from your partner's perspective. While it can be unsettling to face this reflection, it's a crucial step towards deeper understanding and validation. Remember, empathy is a muscle—the more you use it, the stronger it gets.

Exercise: What I Hear You Saying Is...: The Art of Active Validation

Introduction

Have you ever had a conversation where you felt like your words were falling into a black hole? Frustrating, isn't it? Prepare to bridge that cosmic gap with 'What I Hear You Saying Is...'. In this exercise, you'll practice the art of active listening to validate your partner's feelings and thoughts. It's time to make sure your words don't just take a one-way trip to nowhere.

Objective

This exercise aims to enhance your active listening skills, allowing you to reflect your partner's thoughts and feelings accurately. This mutual validation can be a cornerstone of effective communication.

Duration

This exercise requires a dedicated 20-30 minute session. It's like a gym workout for your listening skills—no sweat, all gain.

Materials Needed
- A quiet and comfortable space
- A topic or issue you both agree needs discussion
- Open minds and ears

Instructions
1. **Choose a Topic**: Select a topic or issue that you both agree needs some discussion. Nothing too hot—this isn't the time to solve world peace.

2. **Speaker and Listener:** Designate one partner as the Speaker and the other as the Listener.
3. **Share:** The Speaker shares their thoughts and feelings on the chosen topic.
4. **Paraphrase:** The Listener says, 'What I hear you saying is...' and paraphrases what the Speaker has said. There is no interpreting, just mirroring.
5. **Validation:** The Speaker confirms whether the paraphrasing was accurate. If yes, switch roles. If not, clarify what was missed or misunderstood.
6. **Switch and Repeat:** After the first round, switch roles and repeat the process.

Points for Reflection
- Did paraphrasing help us understand each other better?
- How did it feel to have your words and feelings mirrored back to you?
- Were there any challenges in avoiding interpretation while paraphrasing?

Tips for Success
- Avoid the temptation to add your interpretation or solutions while paraphrasing.
- Keep eye contact to show that you are fully engaged in the conversation.
- If you're the Speaker, try to express your thoughts as clearly as possible to aid the Listener in their task.

Closing Thoughts
'What I Hear You Saying Is...' provides a practical framework for ensuring both partners feel heard and validated. As you make this a regular practice, you'll find that many misunderstandings can be nipped in the bud, creating a smoother, more harmonious relationship.

Exercise: Appreciation Circle- Because Nothing Says 'I Love You' Like Gratitude

Introduction
Who doesn't love a good compliment, right? But let's take it up a notch. Welcome to the Appreciation Circle, where you'll shower each other with praise and learn the art of receiving compliments. Prepare to get all warm and fuzzy inside.

Objective

The aim is to cultivate gratitude and strengthen emotional bonds. It's like emotional weightlifting for your relationship—time to flex those appreciation muscles!

Duration

Set aside 20-30 minutes for this exercise. It's the perfect end-of-week treat—better than Netflix and chill. Trust us.

Materials Needed

- A cozy environment, like your living room
- Your full attention (so maybe not right after a heated episode of your favorite show)

Instructions

1. **Get Comfortable:** Find a quiet and comfortable space where both of you can sit facing each other. Let's get the mood right.
2. **One at a Time:** One partner begins by stating something they appreciate about the other. No cheating—'I appreciate that you're you' is sweet but too easy.
3. **The Receiver:** The other partner listens and then says, 'Thank you,' acknowledging the appreciation without deflecting or downplaying it. No, 'Oh, it was nothing.'
4. **Switch:** Now it's the other partner's turn to give and receive appreciation.
5. **Go for Three:** Try for at least three rounds. It's a circle, not a dot.
6. **Reflect:** Share what it felt like to give and receive appreciation.

Points for Reflection

- How did you feel before and after the exercise?
- Was it easier to give or receive appreciation? Why?
- What did you learn about your partner that you didn't know or hadn't thought about?

Tips for Success

- Be specific with your appreciation. The devil is in the details, but so is the divine.
- Maintain eye contact. It takes the experience from 'meh' to 'wow!'
- Keep it real. Authenticity is the key to making this exercise meaningful.

Closing Thoughts

Gratitude is a gift that keeps on giving. The Appreciation Circle enriches your emotional vocabulary and creates a positive cycle of love and gratitude. Keep this circle going, and you'll find that your relationship becomes a more fulfilling and joyful space.

Exercise: The Validation Journal

Introduction

The joy of journaling—penning down thoughts, doodling in the margins, and, in this case, capturing moments of validation. Welcome to 'The Validation Journal,' an exercise aimed at consciously recognizing and documenting the validating moments in your relationship. Think of it as a scrapbook but for your emotional well-being.

Objective

The goal is to become more aware of the validating behaviors occurring naturally between you and your partner. In doing so, you'll appreciate each other more and understand the kinds of validation that resonate the most.

Duration

This is an ongoing exercise meant to span weeks or even months. Each entry takes a few minutes, but the cumulative effect can be deeply enriching.

Materials Needed
- A physical journal or digital app for journaling
- A pen, if you're going old-school (or a keyboard, for the tech-savvy)
- A shared commitment to notice and appreciate validation

Instructions
1. **Choose the Medium**: Decide whether you'll use a physical journal or a digital app. Make sure it's easily accessible to both of you.
2. **Frequency:** Agree on how often you'll make entries—daily, weekly, or as moments of validation occur.

3. **Log the Moments:** Whenever you experience a validating moment, jot it down in the journal. Please include the date, what was said or done, and how it made you feel.
4. **Review:** Set aside a time to review the journal together, perhaps once a week.
5. **Reflect and Discuss:** Discuss the entries, their meaning to you, and how they contributed to your emotional well-being.

Points for Reflection
- Were there validating moments you hadn't noticed until you started journaling?
- Did the exercise change the frequency or quality of validation in your relationship?
- Were there any surprises or insights gained through this exercise?

Tips for Success
- Be as specific as possible in your entries. The more detail, the better.
- Honesty is key. Log the moments that genuinely felt validating, not just those you think should be validating.
- Keep the journal where both of you can easily access it. Out of sight, out of mind.

Closing Thoughts
Keeping a Validation Journal is a constant reminder of the emotional support in your relationship. It's a tangible testament to the love, respect, and validation you offer each other daily, consciously or unconsciously. Happy journaling!

WEEK 2

Understanding Emotions

Exploring Emotions and Emotional Intelligence in Relationships

Welcome to a transformative journey through the labyrinth of emotions and emotional intelligence. This isn't just a detour in the world of self-help; it's a deep dive into the very core of what makes us human and how that humanity manifests in our relationships. As you open this workbook section, consider it as unlocking a treasure trove of insights that will illuminate your understanding of emotions and empower you to navigate them skillfully.

Importance of Understanding Emotions
Emotions aren't just psychological experiences; they're the language of our inner world. They communicate our deepest needs, fears, desires, and joys. Yet, how often do we misinterpret this language in ourselves or our partners? Understanding emotions is like becoming fluent in this internal language, allowing for a more authentic, empathetic, and enriching relationship.

What is Emotional Intelligence?
Emotional Intelligence is not just a buzzword; it's a multi-faceted skill set that includes recognizing, understanding, managing, and effectively using emotions. It's the 'soft skill' with a hard impact, affecting everything from our intimate relationships to our professional success. It goes beyond IQ and taps into empathy, self-awareness, and emotional regulation, which binds individuals in a meaningful connection.

Objective of the Workbook Section on Emotions
This workbook section aims to be your emotional compass, guiding you through the myriad shades of human emotions, from the simple to the complex, the obvious to the subtle. We'll explore emotional literacy, delve into emotional triggers and responses, and decode the role

of emotional intelligence in relationships. Each chapter offers a blend of theory, real-life scenarios, and actionable tips to apply these insights.

The Emotional Spectrum

Understanding the Range and Diversity of Human Emotions

Emotions are the colors that fill the canvas of our lives. Just like a painter mixes primary colors to create an endless array of hues, our emotional spectrum is a complex blend of basic feelings, each combining uniquely to form our emotional landscape. This chapter will take you on a guided tour through this vibrant world, dissecting the intricacies of human emotions from the simplest to the most complex.

Primary Emotions

These are the building blocks of our emotional experience. Happiness, sadness, fear, anger, surprise, and disgust are often considered the primary colors of the emotional palette. These emotions are universal, crossing cultural and linguistic boundaries. They're hardwired into our biology and serve as our initial emotional responses to stimuli.

Secondary Emotions

When primary emotions combine or evolve, they give rise to secondary emotions. For example, love can be seen as a combination of happiness and trust, while jealousy might emerge from a blend of anger and fear. These emotions are more nuanced and can be influenced by personal experiences, cultural upbringing, and even our thoughts.

Complex Emotions

These are the multi-layered, often conflicting emotions that don't have a simple explanation. They can involve a mixture of primary and secondary emotions and cognitive processes. An example would be 'bittersweet' feelings, where happiness and sadness coexist, often making it challenging to articulate precisely what you're feeling.

Cultural Variations in Emotions

While primary emotions are universal, how they're expressed and experienced can vary widely across cultures. Some cultures have unique words for emotions that don't have direct translations in other languages. For instance, the Japanese term 'Mono no aware' captures the beauty of ephemeral things, a nuanced emotion without a direct English equivalent.

Navigating Your Emotional Landscape

Understanding the emotional spectrum is like having a detailed map of an unexplored territory. It enables you to navigate the highs and lows, the complexities and simplicities of your emotional world with greater ease. Recognizing the diversity of your emotional experiences enriches your self-understanding and improves your interactions with others, making your relationships more fulfilling and authentic.

Emotional Literacy

Learning to Identify and Articulate Emotions Accurately

If emotions are a language, then emotional literacy is fluency in that language. It's not merely about identifying what you feel; it's about understanding the nuances, the subtleties, and the complexities of your emotional experiences. This chapter offers a deep dive into emotional literacy, illustrating why it's crucial and how to develop it.

Benefits of Emotional Literacy

Being emotionally literate is akin to having a GPS for your emotional world. It helps you navigate complex feelings, making it easier to understand yourself and others. This skill is invaluable in relationships, where misunderstandings often stem from misinterpreted emotions. It also enables you to manage your emotions better, contributing to mental well-being and reducing stress.

Barriers to Emotional Literacy

Several factors can inhibit emotional literacy. Cultural norms that stigmatize emotional expression, past traumas that make certain emotions painful, or even a lack of emotional education can be barriers. Understanding these obstacles is the first step in dismantling them.

Strategies for Improving Emotional Literacy

Improving your emotional literacy is like honing any other skill—it takes practice and awareness. Some effective strategies include emotional journaling, where you jot down your feelings and their possible triggers; engaging in mindful meditation to become more aware of your emotional states; and active listening in conversations to understand not just words but the emotions behind them.

The Role of Emotional Literacy in Relationships

Emotional literacy is not just a personal skill; it's a relational one. Accurately identifying and expressing your emotions creates a foundation for empathetic interaction. It can transform relationships from battlegrounds of misunderstood feelings into safe spaces of mutual understanding and respect.

Your Emotional Vocabulary

One practical way to improve emotional literacy is to expand your emotional vocabulary. Instead of labeling a feeling as 'good' or 'bad,' delve deeper. Are you feeling content or ecstatic? Are you anxious or merely concerned? The more precise you are with your emotional descriptors, the better you'll be at understanding the nuances of what you and others feel.

Emotional Literacy as a Lifelong Journey

Becoming emotionally literate is not a one-time achievement; it's a lifelong journey. Like learning a language, the more you practice, the more fluent you become. And the more fluent you are, the richer and more meaningful your relationships become. Emotional literacy is about decoding emotions and enriching your emotional experience.

Emotional Triggers and Responses

Exploring What Triggers Emotional Responses and How to Manage Them

Imagine walking through a minefield, but instead of explosives, it's filled with emotional triggers. One wrong step and—boom!—an eruption of feelings. Emotional triggers are events, words, or experiences that provoke an intense emotional reaction within us. This chapter aims to help you identify your emotional triggers and understand how they prompt specific emotional responses. More importantly, it will provide strategies to manage these triggers effectively.

Common Emotional Triggers

While emotional triggers vary from person to person, some are nearly universal. Criticism, rejection, and feeling excluded can trigger intense emotions in most people. Other triggers might be more personal, linked to specific experiences or traumas, like the anniversary of a painful event or encountering a situation that reminds you of past difficulties.

Emotional Responses and Their Impact

When triggered, our emotional responses can range from anger and aggression to withdrawal and depression. These reactions can significantly impact our well-being and the quality of our relationships. For instance, an aggressive response might lead to conflicts, while withdrawal might create emotional distance between you and your loved ones.

The Underlying Mechanics

Understanding emotional triggers also requires digging deeper into the underlying mechanics. Often, these triggers are tied to unmet needs or unresolved issues. For example, a need for validation might make you sensitive to criticism, or past experiences of betrayal might make trust issues a trigger for you.

Managing Emotional Triggers

Managing triggers isn't about avoiding them but learning to cope with them effectively. Mindfulness techniques can help you become aware of your triggers as they occur, allowing you to choose a different emotional response. Cognitive Behavioral Therapy (CBT) strategies can also be useful in re-framing the thoughts that accompany emotional triggers.

Creating a Personal Trigger Map

One practical exercise is creating a 'Trigger Map,' listing your known emotional triggers and the typical responses they elicit. This map serves as a quick reference guide, helping you anticipate and prepare for situations where you might be triggered.

The Interpersonal Aspect of Triggers

Emotional triggers aren't just a solo affair; they often involve others. Recognizing the triggers that affect you and your partner or loved ones can lead to more empathetic and supportive relationships. It's not just about managing your triggers but understanding theirs as well.

Building Emotional Resilience

Ultimately, managing emotional triggers is about building resilience. The more skilled you become at identifying and coping with triggers, the more emotionally resilient you become. This resilience empowers you and enriches your relationships, turning potential emotional minefields into fields of emotional wisdom.

Emotional Intelligence in Relationships

How Emotional Intelligence Affects the Quality and Dynamics of Relationships

If relationships were a dance, emotional intelligence would be the movement's rhythm. The silent yet powerful undercurrent shapes how we connect, respond, and engage with each other. This chapter delves into the role of emotional intelligence in relationships, dissecting its various components and illustrating how they contribute to healthier, more fulfilling connections.

Empathy

Empathy is the cornerstone of emotional intelligence in relationships. It's the ability to step into someone else's emotional shoes, to feel what they feel, and to understand their perspective. Empathy allows for deeper emotional bonding and is the antidote to misunderstandings and conflicts.

Emotional Regulation

Emotional regulation is another crucial aspect of emotional intelligence: managing and controlling one's emotional reactions. Emotional regulation ensures that your feelings don't overwhelm or negatively affect your interactions. It's like having an emotional thermostat that you can adjust according to the situation's needs.

Self-awareness

Self-awareness is the mirror in the emotional intelligence toolkit. It allows you to see your emotional strengths, weaknesses, triggers, and patterns. This self-knowledge is invaluable in a relationship where understanding yourself helps you understand your partner.

Social Skills

Emotional intelligence extends beyond the personal realm into the social sphere. Social skills such as active listening, conflict resolution, and effective communication are the practical applications of emotional intelligence. These skills can transform the quality of your interactions, not just with your partner but in all your relationships.

Emotional Intelligence as Relationship Capital

Think of emotional intelligence as a form of 'relationship capital.' The more you invest in it, the greater the emotional dividends you reap. It's a resource that enhances not just romantic relationships but friendships, family relations, and even professional connections.

Balancing Emotional Intelligence in a Relationship

Emotional intelligence is not just an individual trait but a collective one in a relationship. It's crucial to balance your emotional intelligence with that of your partner. This balance ensures that one person's emotional needs or reactions don't dominate the relationship, creating a more equitable emotional landscape.

The Transformative Power of Emotional Intelligence

Embracing emotional intelligence can be transformative. It can turn rocky relationships into stable ones, detached interactions into intimate bonds, and mundane conversations into meaningful exchanges. It's not just a skill set; it's a mindset, a way of viewing and engaging with the world that enriches not just you but everyone around you.

Emotional Challenges and How to Overcome Them

Addressing Common Emotional Challenges in Relationships

Navigating the emotional landscape of relationships is like sailing through a sea with varying weather conditions. One moment, it's smooth sailing, and the next, you're in the middle of an emotional storm. This chapter is your navigational guide through these emotional challenges, offering you the tools and insights to weather these storms and emerge stronger.

Emotional Distance

One of the most common emotional challenges in relationships is emotional distance. It's like an invisible wall that separates you from your partner. Emotional distance can result from various factors—from unresolved conflicts to unexpressed feelings. Open communication and a willingness to be vulnerable are the key to overcoming this challenge.

Emotional Vulnerability

While vulnerability is essential for emotional closeness, it can also be a double-edged sword. Being emotionally vulnerable opens you up to potential hurt and disappointment. Yet, it's a risk worth taking. Emotional vulnerability is the gateway to deeper intimacy and understanding. It allows you to be authentic, fostering a relationship based on genuine feelings rather than superficial interactions.

Overcoming Emotional Barriers

Life experiences, past traumas, and even our upbringing can create emotional barriers that make it difficult to connect on a deeper level. These barriers often manifest as defense mechanisms—like avoiding conflict or suppressing emotions. Overcoming these barriers involves recognizing them for what they are and then actively working to dismantle them through self-help strategies or professional guidance.

Emotional Baggage

We all bring emotional baggage into our relationships—past hurts, betrayals, or insecurities. Acknowledging this baggage and its impact on your current relationship is the first step in dealing with it. The next step involves unpacking this baggage by discussing it openly with your partner or seeking therapeutic help.

Emotional Expectations and Realities

Often, emotional challenges arise from the gap between expectations and reality. You might expect emotional support that your partner is unable to provide or wish for a level of emotional intimacy that isn't reciprocated. Realigning these expectations with reality involves honest communication and, sometimes, a willingness to compromise.

Emotional Safety Nets

Building emotional safety nets involves creating a relationship environment where you and your partner feel safe expressing your emotions without judgment. This emotional safety net becomes a foundation upon which you can address and overcome various emotional challenges.

Emotional Resilience as a Relationship Asset

Facing and overcoming emotional challenges in a relationship builds emotional resilience, strengthening your emotional core. It's like building emotional muscles—the more you exercise them, the stronger they become. This resilience becomes valuable, equipping you to handle future emotional challenges in your relationship and life.

The Emotional Journey Ahead

Summarizing the Emotional Insights Gained and Charting the Path Forward

As we reach the final chapter of this workbook, consider it not as an end but as a new beginning—an entry point into a more emotionally enriched life and relationships. You've equipped yourself with the tools, strategies, and insights to navigate the complex world of emotions. But the journey doesn't stop here. The horizon of emotional intelligence is ever-expanding, and this chapter aims to prepare you for the emotional adventures that lie ahead.

Emotional Milestones

Take a moment to reflect on the emotional milestones you've achieved. Perhaps you've better understood your emotional triggers or learned to articulate your feelings more precisely. These milestones, no matter how small, are stepping stones toward becoming more emotionally intelligent.

The Ongoing Quest for Emotional Growth

Emotional intelligence is not a destination; it's an ongoing journey. Like a garden, it requires regular tending—watering the positive emotions, pruning the negative ones, and nourishing the emotional bonds that connect you with others. The quest for emotional growth is a lifetime commitment, but it pays immeasurable dividends in personal happiness and relational fulfillment.

Emotional Skills as Life Skills

The emotional skills you've learned through this workbook are not just for your relationships; they're life skills. They will serve you in various situations, from diffusing conflicts at work to creating stronger bonds with family and friends. Consider them as tools in your emotional toolkit, applicable across the multiple dimensions of your life.

The Emotional Ripple Effect

Your emotional growth doesn't just affect you; it creates a ripple effect, impacting everyone around you. As you become more emotionally intelligent, you foster an environment where emotional literacy and empathy thrive, encouraging others to embark on their emotional journeys.

Keeping the Emotional Flame Alive

Emotional growth is like a flame that needs constant fuel. Continue to invest in your emotional well-being through ongoing learning, mindfulness practices, and open dialogues with your loved ones. Your commitment to keeping this emotional flame alive will ensure that it continues to illuminate your life and relationships.

A Toast to Your Emotional Future

As we close this chapter, here's a toast to your emotional future. May it be filled with the richness of well-understood feelings, the wisdom of well-managed emotions, and the beauty of well-nurtured relationships. Here's to a future where every emotional challenge becomes an opportunity for growth, and every emotional experience is a stepping stone to a better you.

Your Personalized Workbook

> *While this workbook offers a structured approach, it's designed to be flexible. The exercises provided don't have to be taken in the order they are listed. Feel free to pick and choose exercises that resonate with you and are most appropriate for the specific challenges or circumstances you're facing. Consider this workbook as a menu of options, not a set sequence of steps.*

Chapter Exercises

Exercise: The Needs and Fears Inventory

Introduction
Understanding your emotional needs and fears is vital for deeper self-awareness and healthier relationships. The 'Needs and Fears Inventory' exercise aims to help couples explicitly articulate their emotional needs and fears and understand how these can trigger specific emotional reactions.

Objective
This exercise aims to help both partners link their underlying needs and fears to their emotional reactions. This deeper understanding can lead to more empathetic interactions and a stronger emotional connection.

Time Required
30-40 minutes

Materials Needed
- Notebook or journal for each participant
- Writing utensils
- Comfortable seating arrangement

Instructions
1. **Preparation:** Make sure both partners have a notebook or journal and a pen. Sit in a comfortable and quiet space.
2. **Individual Listing:** Individually, write down your top 5 emotional needs and fears. Take about 10 minutes for this step.
3. **Sharing:** Take turns sharing your lists with each other. Listen actively and avoid interrupting while your partner is sharing.

4. **Discussion:** Discuss how the needs and fears listed might trigger specific emotional reactions in different situations. Try to understand the underlying emotional dynamics that could be affecting your relationship.

Supplementary Details
- This exercise aligns with Emotionally Focused Therapy (EFT) principles, focusing on the deeper emotional needs and fears that can affect relational dynamics.
- Revisiting this exercise periodically can be beneficial, as needs and fears may evolve over time.

Tips for Success
- Honesty and vulnerability are essential for the success of this exercise.
- Be supportive and non-judgmental while listening to your partner's needs and fears.
- Use this exercise as a starting point for an ongoing emotional needs and fears dialogue.

Potential Pitfalls
- Misinterpretation: It's easy to misunderstand the emotional weight of certain needs or fears if not adequately explained.
- Emotional Overwhelm: The discussion might bring up strong emotions. Handle these sensitively and consider taking a break if needed.

Exercise: Emotional Hot Seat

Introduction
Real-time emotional identification and regulation are crucial skills for maintaining healthy relationships and mental well-being. The 'Emotional Hot Seat' exercise provides a controlled environment for couples to practice these skills by reacting to hypothetical situations.

Objective
The main objective of this exercise is to practice identifying and regulating emotions in real time. This can help individuals become more aware of their emotional triggers and learn effective ways to manage them.

Time Required
15-20 minutes

Materials Needed
- A list of hypothetical situations that could trigger emotional responses
- Comfortable seating arrangement

Instructions
1. **Preparation:** Sit in a comfortable space where both of you can focus. Have a list of hypothetical situations ready that are likely to elicit an emotional response.
2. **Scenario Presentation:** One partner picks a hypothetical situation from the list and describes it to the other partner.
3. **Immediate Identification:** The listening partner identifies their immediate emotional response to the hypothetical situation. Try to be as specific as possible.
4. **Regulation Strategy:** The listening partner then suggests a healthy way to manage or regulate the identified emotion.
5. **Role Reversal:** Switch roles and repeat steps 2-4. Continue alternating roles until you've gone through several scenarios.

Supplementary Details
- This exercise incorporates Cognitive Behavioral Therapy (CBT) principles by encouraging immediate emotional identification and cognitive restructuring.
- The exercise can be more challenging by increasing the complexity or sensitivity of the hypothetical situations.

Tips for Success
- Honesty is crucial for the success of this exercise. Authentic emotional responses provide the most valuable insights.
- Take your time with each scenario; the aim is not to rush through but to deeply understand your emotional triggers and coping mechanisms.

Potential Pitfalls
- Superficial Responses: The exercise might be less effective if you give socially desirable or superficial responses instead of authentic emotional reactions.

- Emotional Overwhelm: If the exercise triggers strong emotions, consider pausing and discussing those feelings openly or seeking professional guidance.

Exercise: Emotional Safety Net

Introduction
Creating a safe emotional environment is paramount for the health and longevity of any relationship. The 'Emotional Safety Net' exercise aims to help couples identify the actions or words that contribute to emotional safety or lack thereof. By understanding these triggers, couples can create a 'safety plan' to foster a more secure emotional connection.

Objective
This exercise aims to enable couples to explicitly communicate their needs and boundaries to create a safe emotional space for each other.

Time Required
30-45 minutes

Materials Needed
- Notebook or journal for each participant
- Writing utensils
- Comfortable seating arrangement

Instructions
1. **Preparation:** Make sure both partners have a notebook or journal and a pen. Choose a quiet, comfortable space where you can talk openly without distractions.
2. **Discussion:** Discuss what actions, words, or situations make you feel emotionally safe or unsafe in your relationship.
3. **Listing:** Individually write down the points discussed. Try to be as specific as possible.
4. **Safety Plan:** Create a 'safety plan' based on your discussion and lists. This plan should include actionable steps to foster emotional safety.
5. **Review and Commit:** Review the 'safety plan' together and commit to implementing it daily.

Supplementary Details
- This exercise incorporates Emotionally Focused Therapy (EFT) concepts by emphasizing the importance of attachment and emotional safety.
- The 'safety plan' should be revisited and updated regularly to adapt to changes or new insights.

Tips for Success
- Honesty and vulnerability are crucial for the success of this exercise.
- This is a judgment-free zone; the objective is to understand each other's needs and not to criticize.
- If some topics are too sensitive to handle without guidance, consider involving a professional.

Potential Pitfalls
- Avoidance: Skipping or avoiding sensitive topics might result in an incomplete or ineffective safety plan.
- Implementation: The exercise is only as effective as its implementation. Both partners must be committed to putting the plan into action.

Exercise: Recognizing Destructive Communication Patterns

Introduction
Communication is the backbone of any relationship, but not all forms of communication are constructive. The 'Recognizing Destructive Communication Patterns' exercise aims to help couples identify specific negative communication habits—namely Criticism, Defensiveness, Stonewalling, and Contempt—that can hinder emotional connection and overall relationship health.

Objective
This exercise aims to help couples recognize and understand destructive communication patterns in their interactions. Identifying these patterns is the first step toward healthier communication and a stronger emotional connection.

Time Required
20-30 minutes

Materials Needed
- Notebook or journal for each participant
- Writing utensils
- Comfortable seating arrangement

Instructions
1. **Preparation:** Each partner should have a notebook or journal and a pen. Sit facing each other in a comfortable, distraction-free environment.
2. **Recall:** Each partner should independently recall a recent argument or heated discussion. Write down the main points and your reactions during the conversation.
3. **Identification:** Review your notes and try to identify instances where either you or your partner displayed Criticism, Defensiveness, Stonewalling, or Contempt.
4. **Sharing:** Take turns sharing your observations. Discuss openly, but avoid blaming or criticizing each other for the negative patterns.
5. **Reflection and Planning:** Reflect on how these destructive patterns have impacted your relationship and plan actionable steps to improve communication.

Supplementary Details
- Understanding the presence of these destructive communication patterns can lead to more effective communication and a stronger emotional connection.
- The exercise can be repeated periodically to monitor improvement and make necessary adjustments.

Tips for Success
- Honesty and openness are crucial for the success of this exercise.
- If the discussion becomes too heated or counterproductive, take a break and revisit it when emotions have cooled down.
- Be solution-oriented rather than focusing on blame.

Potential Pitfalls
- Defensive Reactions: The exercise might trigger defensiveness if not approached sensitively.

- Incomplete Analysis: Skipping the planning step could result in an incomplete exercise, lacking actionable outcomes.

Exercise: Emotional Reactions Role-Play

Introduction
Understanding emotions is one thing, but recognizing them as they happen in real-time scenarios is a challenge. The 'Emotional Reactions Role-Play' exercise is designed to help couples become more adept at identifying emotional triggers and formulating healthier responses.

Objective
The main objective of this exercise is to practice recognizing emotional triggers and reactions in a controlled environment. This enables couples to be better prepared for real-life situations.

Time Required
30-45 minutes

Materials Needed
- A list of scenarios that are emotionally charged for both partners
- Comfortable seating arrangement
- A timer

Instructions
1. **Preparation:** Sit together in a comfortable space where you won't be disturbed. Have a list of emotionally charged scenarios ready.
2. **Scenario Selection:** One partner selects a scenario from the list to enact.
3. **Role-Play:** Both partners act out the chosen scenario. Try to make it as realistic as possible.
4. **Pause and Reflect:** Use a timer to pause the role-play every 3-5 minutes. Each partner should take a moment to identify their emotional state.
5. **Discuss:** Share your identified emotions. Discuss what triggered these emotions and how you could respond differently.

6. **Resume or Switch:** Either resume the current role-play or switch to a new scenario, and repeat steps 3-5.
7. **Wrap-up:** After completing a couple of scenarios, discuss what you've learned and how you can apply these insights in real-life situations.

Supplementary Details

- This exercise incorporates elements from Cognitive Behavioral Therapy by encouraging the identification of emotional triggers and exploring alternative, healthier emotional responses.
- You may want to make this a regular practice to improve your emotional intelligence and response mechanisms continuously.

Tips for Success

- Honesty is crucial. Don't downplay your emotions for the sake of your partner's feelings.
- Use the timer strictly to ensure that the exercise remains structured.
- It might be beneficial to revisit the same scenarios after some time to gauge progress.

Potential Pitfalls

- Escalation: If emotions run high and the exercise becomes counterproductive, it may be best to pause and seek professional guidance.
- Misidentification: The exercise may be less effective if partners are not honest or accurate in identifying their emotions.

Exercise: The Emotional Inventory

Introduction

Emotions are the cornerstone of human experience, shaping our interactions, choices, and well-being. Understanding emotions—both your own and your partner's—can be the key to long-lasting connection and happiness. "The Emotional Inventory" aims to enhance emotional intelligence and attunement between couples by providing a structured way to identify, articulate, and discuss emotional experiences.

Objective

This exercise aims to deepen your understanding of your emotional landscape and that of your partner. Couples can foster empathy and strengthen emotional bonds by sharing and labeling emotions.

Time Required

20-30 minutes

Materials Needed

- Notebook or journal for each participant
- Writing utensils
- Comfortable seating arrangement

Instructions

1. **Preparation:** Each partner should have a notebook or journal and a pen. Sit facing each other in a comfortable, distraction-free environment.
2. **Identification:** Take a few moments to reflect on an emotional event you experienced in the past week. This could be related to work, family, or the relationship itself.
3. **Sharing:** One partner begins by sharing details of their emotional event. Focus on describing what happened, how it made you feel, and why you think it triggered such emotions.
4. **Active Listening:** The listening partner should remain attentive, making mental notes but not interrupting the storytelling.
5. **Labeling:** After the first partner has finished sharing, the listening partner attempts to label the described emotions. Use specific terms like 'anxious,' 'joyful,' 'resentful,' etc.
6. **Discussion:** Open the floor for a brief discussion about the accuracy of the labeling. Did the listening partner get it right? If not, what were the missing elements?
7. **Role Reversal:** Switch roles and repeat steps 2-6.
8. **Wrap-up:** Conclude by summarizing what you have learned about each other's emotional experiences and discussing ways to be more attuned in the future.

Supplementary Details

- This exercise incorporates principles from the Gottman Method by focusing on emotional attunement and understanding.
- Couples can make this a regular practice, perhaps once a week, to stay emotionally connected.
- If either partner has difficulty identifying an emotional event, consider scenarios that elicit strong emotions, such as receiving praise or criticism, making significant decisions, or facing challenges.

Tips for Success

- Maintain eye contact and open body language during the exercise.
- Avoid judgment or criticism; this is a safe space to share and understand.
- If you find that certain emotions are recurrent, exploring them further in future sessions or with professional guidance may be helpful.

Potential Pitfalls

- Oversimplifying emotions: Emotions can be complex and multifaceted. Be open to the possibility that more than one emotion could be in play.
- Emotional withdrawal: If the exercise triggers strong emotional responses, handling them sensitively is crucial. Consider taking a break or seeking professional assistance.

Identifying Negative Interaction Patterns

Navigating the Labyrinth of Love and Conflict

Ah, love—the eternal dance of intimacy and intricacy, where two souls attempt to move harmoniously while avoiding stepping on each other's toes. If only it were that simple, right? Welcome to the workbook that aims to be your relationship's dance instructor, teaching you the steps to evade those proverbial missteps and twirls that lead to emotional sprains and strains.

You're here because you've realized love isn't just about heart emojis and candle-lit dinners. It's also about navigating the maze of emotions, reactions, and yes, the dreaded negative interaction patterns that can turn your romantic waltz into a chaotic jumble. It's as if someone switched the music from a romantic ballad to heavy metal without warning. Not that there's anything wrong with heavy metal, but headbanging isn't exactly conducive to a slow dance!

Why Negative Interaction Patterns?
Why focus on the negatives, you ask? We're not pessimists but realists with a sprinkle of optimism. Negative interaction patterns are like potholes on the road to relationship bliss. They jolt you, can damage your 'vehicle,' and make the journey less enjoyable. By identifying and understanding these patterns, we're handing you a shovel and some asphalt to fill those potholes in.

What to Expect?
This workbook is divided into thoughtfully designed sections, each targeting a different facet of negative interactions—from understanding the cycle to linking your internal reactions to actions. It's like a relationship Swiss Army knife, versatile and practical.

Emotional Intelligence: Your Secret Weapon

We're also introducing emotional intelligence as your relationship's secret weapon. Think of it as your relationship's sixth sense, helping you navigate the fog of misunderstandings and emotional outbursts. And no, you don't have to be a psychic to develop this sense. We'll guide you through it.

The Path Forward

As you progress through the chapters, we encourage you to be open, vulnerable, and, most importantly, honest—first with yourself and then with your partner. After all, the first step to solving any problem is admitting there is one, right?

Understanding the Cycle of Negative Interactions

Ah, the cycle of negative interactions—sometimes it feels like a merry-go-round that's lost its 'merry,' doesn't it? The cycle starts, spirals, and before you know it, both of you are dizzy from the emotional ups and downs. But don't worry, we're here to put the brakes on this ride and help you understand how to disembark safely.

Triggers that Start the Cycle

Have you ever wondered why a simple question like 'What's for dinner?' can sometimes ignite a full-blown argument? Welcome to the world of triggers—those seemingly innocent words, actions, or expressions that set off emotional fireworks. Understanding your and your partner's triggers is the first step in breaking the cycle of negative interactions.

Triggers are deeply personal and often rooted in past experiences, fears, or insecurities. It's like each person carries an invisible emotional 'minefield,' and knowing where not to step can make all the difference. For some, it could be a tone of voice that reminds them of a critical parent. For others, it could be a certain phrase that brings back memories of past betrayal. The key is to map out these emotional minefields and carefully navigate them.

The Role of Communication in Perpetuating the Cycle

Ah, communication—the 'magical' tool that can either mend bridges or blow them up! When it comes to the cycle of negative interactions, how you communicate plays a colossal role. Have you ever heard of the term 'It's not what you say; it's how you say it?' Well, there's profound wisdom in those words.

Let's start with the basics. Communication isn't just about exchanging information; it's also about understanding the emotional subtext behind the words. It's like an iceberg; the tip represents the words spoken, and the massive structure beneath the surface represents the emotions, intentions, and unspoken expectations. Missing the latter is like sailing blindly into treacherous waters.

Poor communication habits can reinforce the cycle of negative interactions. Whether it's interrupting when your partner is speaking, using accusatory language, or assuming rather than asking—these are all recipes for a communication disaster. The cycle continues because instead of resolving issues, poor communication adds more fuel to the emotional fire.

So, what's the way out? Awareness and mindfulness in communication can be your guiding stars. Being aware of not just what you're saying but also how you're saying it can change the course of your interaction. Mindfulness helps you pause and think before you speak, ensuring that your words reflect your intentions and not just your immediate emotional state.

In this workbook, we'll dive deeper into enhancing your communication skills and emotional intelligence to break the cycle of negative interactions. But for now, understanding the cycle is half the battle won. The other half? Well, stick around, and we'll get there.

The Root of Negative Interactions

If you've ever pulled weeds from a garden, you know it's not enough to snip them at the surface. You've got to dig deep and pull them out by the root. Negative interactions in relationships are somewhat like those pesky weeds; dealing with them superficially only offers temporary relief. To truly resolve the issue, you've got to dig down to the root cause. So, let's grab our metaphorical shovels and start digging, shall we?

Influence of Past Relationships

Let's face it—none of us come into a relationship as blank slates. We're like walking, talking collages of our past experiences, relationships, and, yes, emotional baggage. These past relationships, whether with family, friends, or former romantic partners, shape our expectations, fears, and reactions in our current relationships.

For instance, if you've been in a relationship where your trust was betrayed, you might be hyper-vigilant about signs of deceit in your current relationship. While it's a natural defense mechanism, it can also be a root cause of negative interactions. Your partner may feel unjustly accused or under constant scrutiny, leading to tension and arguments.

The first step to uprooting this cause is self-awareness. Recognizing how your past is influencing your present can be incredibly liberating. And don't just stop at recognition—communicate these insights with your partner. It's a vulnerable but vital conversation that can set the stage for deeper emotional intimacy.

Unresolved Emotional Issues

Emotional baggage—the 'gift' that keeps on giving, usually in the form of negative interactions. Unresolved emotional issues are like landmines in your emotional landscape; you never know when they'll go off, but you can be sure they'll create a mess when they do.

These issues could range from insecurities about your self-worth to deep-seated fears of abandonment. And the tricky part? Sometimes you don't even realize they exist until they're triggered. It's like discovering a hidden trapdoor in a room you thought you knew well.

Resolving these issues often involves an inward journey, possibly supplemented by professional therapy. It's about reconciling with your past, forgiving where needed (including yourself), and rebuilding your emotional foundation. It's not an overnight process, but it's crucial for breaking the cycle of negative interactions.

We'll delve into various tools and exercises to help you explore and address these root causes. But remember, the journey of a thousand miles begins with a single step—or in this case, a single conversation.

So, as you turn the pages of this workbook, think of it as tilling the soil of your emotional garden. Each chapter, each exercise, is an opportunity to uproot a weed and plant something beautiful in its place. Ready to garden?

Emotional Intelligence and Negative Interaction Patterns

When it comes to relationships, having a high IQ is great, but having a high EQ (Emotional Quotient) is the real game-changer. Think of Emotional Intelligence as the operating system that runs the software of your relationship. It determines how smoothly the programs (read: interactions) execute and how effectively bugs (read: conflicts) are resolved. So, let's delve into the fascinating world of Emotional Intelligence and discover how it can help us break negative interaction patterns.

Lack of Empathy as a Negative Pattern

Empathy is the crown jewel of Emotional Intelligence. It's the ability to understand and share the feelings of another. But what happens when this crucial component is missing or malfunctioning? It's like trying to sail a ship without a compass; you're bound to hit rocky waters.

Lack of empathy leads to a disconnect between partners. You become like two actors in a play, reciting your lines but missing the emotional nuance behind them. This absence of emotional resonance can turn even mundane conversations into breeding grounds for misunderstanding and conflict.

So, how do you cultivate empathy? It starts with active listening, being fully present in conversations, and validating your partner's feelings. It's not just about hearing; it's about understanding. It's looking into your partner's eyes and seeing the soul behind them.

Emotional Self-Regulation

Imagine if every time your partner said something that irked you, you reacted impulsively. Let's just say you'd spend more time arguing than enjoying each other's company. Emotional self-regulation is your internal 'pause' button. It gives you the space to breathe, think, and respond rather than react.

Why is this crucial? Because impulsive reactions are often the catalysts for negative interaction patterns. They are the sparks that ignite the fire of conflict, fueling a cycle of misunderstanding, hurt, and resentment.

As discussed in previous chapters, mastering emotional self-regulation involves recognizing your emotional triggers and developing coping mechanisms. These small acts can make a significant difference, whether taking deep breaths, counting to ten, or even stepping away momentarily.

The following workbook sections will provide practical exercises and tools to enhance your Emotional Intelligence. We'll explore strategies for cultivating empathy, mastering emotional self-regulation, and other key components of Emotional Intelligence.

So, as you flip through the coming pages, remember: Emotional Intelligence is not just an innate talent; it's a skill that can be developed. And much like any skill, the more you practice, the better you get. Are you ready to level up your Emotional Intelligence and transform your relationship?

Common Negative Interaction Patterns

Let's face it: nobody's perfect—especially in relationships. We all have our quirks, idiosyncrasies, and yes, those vexing habits that our partners wish came with an 'off' switch. But while some of these quirks add flavor to the relationship, others become patterns of interaction that are anything but appetizing. In this chapter, we'll explore some common negative interaction patterns that might add a bitter taste to your romantic dish.

Must Always Be 'Right'
The need to always be 'right' can be like a termite in the wooden structure of your relationship. On the surface, everything looks solid, but inside, the need for one-upmanship is eroding the foundation. This pattern stifles open communication and creates an atmosphere where one partner feels devalued or unheard.

The irony is that the need to be 'right' often stems from insecurity and a fear of vulnerability. Admitting you're wrong might feel like exposing a chink in your armor, but in reality, it strengthens your relationship by fostering trust and openness.

Aren't Sensitive to the Emotions of Others
A relationship isn't a solo performance; it's a duet. And like any good duet, it requires attuning to your part and your partner's. A lack of emotional sensitivity can make interactions feel one-sided, creating resentment and widening the emotional gap between you.

Being emotionally insensitive can often be an unconscious pattern, a learned behavior from past experiences or environments where emotional expression was discouraged or devalued. The good news? Patterns that are learned can be unlearned.

Act Inappropriately
Inappropriateness in a relationship can manifest in various ways—from making insensitive jokes to crossing boundaries. Such behavior can create a toxic atmosphere where one partner feels disrespected or unsafe.

Acting inappropriately often stems from a lack of awareness or understanding of your partner's boundaries and comfort zones. It's akin to dancing on a tightrope without realizing how high you are from the ground. The solution? Open, candid conversations about boundaries and appropriate behavior.

Playing the Victim

Ah, the 'victim card,' an all-too-common trump card in negative interactions. Playing the victim shifts the responsibility and blame onto the other person, stifling any productive resolution to conflicts. While it may offer a temporary sense of moral high ground, it builds a mountain of unresolved issues.

This pattern often has roots in past experiences where playing the victim had some 'benefits'—like receiving attention or avoiding responsibility. But in an adult relationship, it's a tactic that quickly loses its charm.

Prone to Emotional Outbursts

Relationships are emotional roller coasters, but if your ride has more downs than ups because of emotional outbursts, it's time for maintenance. Frequent emotional outbursts can make your partner feel like they're walking on eggshells, creating a tense environment.

Emotional outbursts often result from pent-up feelings or unresolved issues. Think of it as steam building up in a pressure cooker. The solution is finding healthy emotional expression outlets and tackling the underlying issues head-on.

We will look at strategies to break these negative interaction patterns in the coming chapters. For now, the first step is acknowledgment. It takes courage to look in the mirror and recognize these patterns, but self-awareness is the first step toward change. Ready to take that step?

Link Your Internal Reaction to Your Action

If relationships are the dance floors of our lives, our internal reactions and subsequent actions are our dance steps. Sometimes, these steps perfectly sync with the music, creating a harmonious performance. At other times, they are out of tune, leading to a more awkward shuffle than a graceful waltz dance. In this chapter, we will explore the connection between your internal reactions and actions, offering insights into how they influence the choreography of your relationship.

Repression: The Silent Killer

Repressing emotions is like sweeping dust under the rug; it might make the surface look clean, but it doesn't solve the underlying issue. Over time, this emotional dust accumulates and becomes a breeding ground for resentment, misunderstanding, and those dreaded negative interaction patterns.

Repression often stems from a fear of confrontation or a misguided belief that emotions are a sign of weakness. But remember, emotions are the language of your inner world, and repressing them is akin to muting your voice.

Denial: The Rose-Colored Glasses

Denial is the psychological equivalent of rose-colored glasses. It's seeing what you want rather than what's there. While it might offer temporary comfort, it distorts reality and hampers authentic communication.

Denial is often a defense mechanism to avoid painful truths or uncomfortable confrontations. However, ignoring a problem doesn't make it disappear; it merely postpones the inevitable reckoning.

Projection: The Emotional Mirror

Projection is like looking in a mirror, but instead of seeing your reflection, you see your emotions and traits reflected onto your partner. You attribute to them feelings or intentions that are your own. The danger here is that it can create conflicts based on illusions rather than facts.

Projection often happens subconsciously and can be a way to deflect personal responsibility. Recognizing this pattern involves a deep dive into self-awareness, often requiring you to confront uncomfortable truths about yourself.

Rationalization: The Master of Excuses

Rationalization is the art of making excuses. It's the narrative you create to justify your actions, especially those that lead to negative interactions. While rationalizing might soothe your conscience in the short term, it prevents genuine understanding and resolution of issues.

The first step to breaking this pattern is brutal honesty—first with yourself and then with your partner. It involves acknowledging your flaws and mistakes without hiding behind the shield of rationalizations.

Displacement and Sublimation: The Emotional Shape-shifters
Displacement involves redirecting emotions from their source to another target. For example, if you're angry at your boss, you might displace that anger onto your partner. Sublimation is a more refined form of displacement where you channel negative emotions into socially acceptable actions or hobbies.

While these mechanisms can offer temporary relief, they don't address the root cause of your emotions. They're like applying a Band-Aid to a wound that needs stitches.

In the coming chapters, we will explore practical exercises and techniques to address these patterns. But for now, understanding the link between your internal reactions and actions is a significant step in changing the dance steps of your relationship. Are you ready to learn some new moves?

Establishing Emotionally Mature Romantic Connections

Love may be a universal language but it comes with various dialects, idioms, and even tricky pronunciations. And one of the most complex yet rewarding dialects to master is that of emotionally mature romantic connections. In this chapter, we'll explore how to cultivate a relationship where both partners are emotionally attuned, respectful, and, most importantly, mature. Because, let's be honest, adulting is hard, but 'relationshipping' as an adult? That's a whole new level.

Tell Your Partner How You Feel
Sounds simple, right? But you'd be surprised how often this basic principle is overlooked. Openly expressing your feelings isn't just about airing your grievances; it's also about sharing your joys, fears, and even your mundane daily experiences. Emotional maturity involves creating a safe space where both partners can be authentic, warts and all.

Telling your partner how you feel goes beyond just verbal expression; it's also about transparency in your actions. It's giving that extra hug when you know they've had a rough day or leaving a sweet note just because. These small acts of emotional expression lay the foundation for a robust emotional connection.

Give Your Partner the Love and Support They Require
Emotional maturity is often equated with self-sufficiency, but let's debunk that myth here. Being emotionally mature doesn't mean you don't need love and support; it means you understand how to give and receive it in a balanced way.

Supporting your partner isn't just about being their cheerleader; it's also about knowing when to step back and allow them their space. It's a delicate dance between being present and being overbearing, and mastering it requires attentiveness and, you guessed it, emotional maturity.

Ask If You're Unsure

The hallmark of an emotionally mature relationship is open communication, including asking questions when you're unsure. No one is a mind reader, and expecting your partner to understand your thinking is unfair and unrealistic.

Whether it's clarifying a statement they made or seeking to understand their feelings on a specific issue, asking questions is a sign of engagement and interest. It shows that you value the relationship enough to seek understanding rather than make assumptions.

Discover Your Partner

Ah, the joy of discovery! Like an explorer setting foot on uncharted land, discovering your partner is an ongoing adventure. And like any adventure, it comes with its share of surprises, challenges, and treasures.

Discovery in an emotionally mature relationship goes beyond just learning their favorite food or movie; it's about understanding their dreams, fears, and how they view the world. It's about peeling back the layers to find the core of the person you love.

In this workbook, we'll guide you through exercises and strategies to help you cultivate an emotionally mature romantic connection. But remember, emotional maturity is not a destination; it's a journey. And it's a journey best undertaken with open hearts, open minds, and perhaps a little dash of humor. Ready to take the first step?

Managing Emotional Triggers in Relationships

We all have those little (or sometimes big) buttons that, when pushed, can turn us from a calm, rational human into an emotional whirlwind. They're called triggers and can wreak havoc in relationships if not managed effectively. In this chapter, let's delve into the world of emotional triggers, understand their origins, and learn strategies to keep them in check. Because let's face it, no one wants to be a ticking emotional time bomb in their relationship.

Understanding the Nature of Triggers

Emotional triggers are like invisible tripwires; you don't know they exist until you've stumbled upon them. They are often rooted in past experiences, traumas, or deeply ingrained beliefs. And while the trigger might seem trivial to an outsider (or even your partner), the emotional response can be intense and overwhelming.

The first step in managing triggers is identifying them. This might require introspection and perhaps a few uncomfortable walks down memory lane. But understanding the 'why' behind the 'what' is crucial for effective management.

Common Triggers and Their Origins

Triggers can vary from person to person, but some common ones include feeling disrespected, invalidated, or ignored. The origins of these triggers often lie in past relationships or childhood experiences where these emotions were prevalent.

For instance, if you grew up in a household where your opinions were often dismissed, you might be triggered by similar behavior in your relationship. Recognizing this link between past experiences and current reactions is essential for breaking the cycle.

The Role of Communication in Trigger Management

Managing triggers isn't a solo endeavor; it's a team sport. Open, honest communication with your partner about your triggers is essential. And this isn't just a one-time conversation; it's an ongoing dialogue.

Because triggers can be touchy subjects, approaching the conversation sensitively is crucial. It's not about blaming your partner for pushing your buttons; it's about helping them understand those buttons and why they exist.

Strategies for Self-Regulation

While communication is key, the responsibility for managing your triggers ultimately lies with you. Self-regulation strategies like deep breathing, taking a 'time-out,' or even seeking professional help can effectively keep your triggers in check.

Strategies for Breaking Negative Interaction Patterns

Okay, so you've identified the negative interaction patterns in your relationship, and you've learned about emotional triggers. Great job! Identifying the problem is half the battle. But what about the other half? How do you go from understanding these patterns to breaking them? Hold on to your emotional seatbelts because, in this chapter, we're diving into the strategies for transforming those negative cycles into positive interactions.

The Importance of Self-Awareness

Think of self-awareness as the GPS of your emotional journey. It helps you identify where you are, where you want to go, and the most effective route. Developing self-awareness involves tuning in to your feelings, thoughts, and behaviors in the context of your relationship.

It may involve journaling, practicing mindfulness, or taking a few moments each day to check in with yourself. Whatever method you choose, the goal is to observe your emotional landscape.

Active Listening: The Unsung Hero

Active listening is communicating what rhythm is to dance. It's not just about hearing the words but understanding the emotions and intentions behind them. This involves listening with your ears, eyes (body language), and heart (empathy).

Practicing active listening can be challenging, especially when emotions run high. It involves putting your thoughts and judgments on hold to engage with your partner's perspective fully. But trust us, the rewards are well worth the effort.

Emotional Validation: The Healing Touch

Validation doesn't mean you agree with your partner; you acknowledge their feelings and perspectives as legitimate. Emotional validation is like a balm for wounds inflicted by negative interaction patterns.

Validation can be as simple as saying, 'I understand how you feel,' or as complex as acknowledging the nuances in your partner's emotional narrative. It's a skill that takes practice but pays off in emotional dividends.

Setting and Respecting Boundaries

Boundaries are the emotional and physical perimeters that define your comfort zone. Setting and respecting boundaries is crucial for breaking negative interaction patterns. This involves clear communication about what behaviors are acceptable and what crosses the line.

It's important to remember that boundaries are not walls but guidelines. And like any good guideline, they can be negotiated and adjusted as the relationship evolves.

Using 'I' Statements for Constructive Communication

'You always do this,' 'You never listen to me,'—sound familiar? These 'you' statements can be triggers for defensive reactions. Switching to 'I' statements like 'I feel hurt when...' or 'I would appreciate if...' changes the dynamic from accusatory to constructive.

In the next sections of this workbook, we'll delve deeper into each of these strategies, providing practical exercises to put them into action. But for now, consider this chapter your strategic overview—a roadmap for transforming your relationship. Ready to hit the road?

Creating a Safe Emotional Space in Your Relationship

The concept of a 'safe space' has been buzzing around social and emotional discussions for a while now. But what does it mean to create a safe emotional space within the intimate quarters of a romantic relationship? In this chapter, we're delving into the elements constituting such a sanctuary of emotional well-being, where both partners can feel valued, understood, and, most importantly, safe.

The Pillars of Emotional Safety

A safe emotional space is built on trust, openness, and mutual respect. These aren't just buzzwords but the foundational stones upon which your emotional haven will stand. Trust is earned, openness is nurtured, and mutual respect is a non-negotiable term of relational engagement.

Navigating Emotional Vulnerabilities

Every person comes with an emotional backstory—past experiences, wounds, and triggers that shape their emotional responses. Recognizing and navigating these vulnerabilities is vital to creating a safe emotional space.

This involves not using these vulnerabilities against your partner during conflicts and validating their feelings even when you don't fully understand them. It's about creating an environment where both partners can expose their emotional underbelly without fearing judgment or ridicule.

The Power of Non-verbal Communication

Words are powerful, but sometimes silence speaks volumes. Non-verbal communication, like eye contact, touch, and even your tone, can convey a depth of emotion that words might fail to capture.

Small gestures like holding hands during a difficult conversation or maintaining eye contact when expressing your feelings can go a long way in creating a safe emotional space. They are the silent narrators of your emotional story, filling in the gaps where words fall short.

Emotional Check-ins: The Regular Tune-ups

Creating a safe emotional space isn't a one-time event; it requires regular maintenance. Think of emotional check-ins as the regular tune-ups that keep your relational engine running smoothly.

These check-ins can be as formal as a designated 'talk time' each week or as casual as asking, 'How are you feeling today?' The key is to make them a consistent practice, ensuring that both partners are in sync and that the emotional space remains safe and nurturing.

The No-Blame Game

In a safe emotional space, blame has no room. The focus shifts from 'Who is at fault?' to 'How can we resolve this?' It's a collaborative effort where both partners are invested in finding solutions rather than pointing fingers.

In the upcoming sections of this workbook, we'll explore exercises and techniques to help you build and maintain a safe emotional space in your relationship. But for now, consider this chapter as your blueprint for constructing an emotional sanctuary where love, understanding, and respect can flourish. Are you ready to pick up the emotional bricks and mortar?

The Role of Empathy in Transforming Negative Interaction Patterns

If emotional intelligence is the 'EQ' of your relationship, consider empathy its beating heart. Empathy—the ability to understand and share the feelings of another—is a transformative power in any relationship, particularly in romantic partnerships. This chapter will explore how empathy can be your secret weapon in turning negative interaction patterns into positive, fulfilling exchanges.

The Anatomy of Empathy

Empathy isn't just a feel-good term; it's a complex emotional skill that involves several components: cognitive empathy (understanding someone else's perspective), emotional empathy (feeling what someone else feels), and compassionate empathy (taking action based on your understanding and feelings).

The trifecta of 'understanding, feeling, and acting' makes empathy potent in relationships. And the good news? It's a skill that can be nurtured and developed.

Empathy as a Communication Bridge

Effective communication isn't just about transmitting your thoughts and feelings; it's also about receiving your partner's messages with an empathic ear. Empathy acts as a bridge that converts simple exchanges into meaningful interactions.

When you approach conversations with an empathic mindset, you're not just hearing the words; you're also picking up on the emotional undertones, the unspoken needs, and the hidden fears. This level of engagement transforms communication from a transaction into a connection.

Empathy and Emotional Safety

Empathy is a cornerstone in the foundation of a safe emotional space. It's saying, 'I see you, I hear you, and what you're feeling matters to me.' This validation creates an atmosphere of emotional safety where each partner feels seen and valued.

When both partners practice empathy, it acts as a buffer against the fallout of emotional triggers and negative interaction patterns. It doesn't make the challenges disappear but makes them easier to navigate.

The Pitfalls of Empathy Burnout

While empathy is a powerful tool, it's also important to wield it wisely. Empathy burnout—feeling emotionally drained from taking on your partner's emotions—can be a real issue. Setting emotional boundaries is crucial to ensure that empathy enhances your relationship rather than depleting your emotional resources.

In the upcoming sections of this workbook, we'll provide exercises to help you cultivate empathy and integrate it into your relationship dynamics. But for now, consider this chapter as your guide to unlocking the transformative power of empathy in your relationship. Are you ready to open your heart?

Your Personalized Workbook

> *While this workbook offers a structured approach, it's designed to be flexible. The exercises provided don't have to be taken in the order they are listed. Feel free to pick and choose exercises that resonate with you and are most appropriate for the specific challenges or circumstances you're facing. Consider this workbook as a menu of options, not a set sequence of steps.*

Chapter Exercises

Exercise: Pattern Identification in Relationships

Introduction

Understanding the dynamics of negative interaction patterns, such as stonewalling or blaming, is critical for relationship health and personal well-being. The 'Pattern Identification' exercise offers a structured approach for couples to recognize and discuss these common negative patterns.

Objective

The primary objective of this exercise is to help couples identify which negative interaction patterns they commonly engage in. This awareness is the first step toward replacing these patterns with healthier communication behaviors.

Time Required

Approximately 30 minutes

Materials Needed

- A list of common negative interaction patterns (e.g., stonewalling, blaming, criticizing, defensiveness)
- Pen and paper for each participant
- Comfortable seating arrangement

Instructions

1. Preparation: Sit in a comfortable and quiet space without being disturbed. Each partner should have a pen and paper.
2. Introduction of Patterns: Present the list of common negative interaction patterns. Take a moment to explain each one briefly.
3. Individual Reflection: Both partners should take 5-10 minutes to jot down instances where they've noticed these patterns in their relationship. Try to be as specific as possible.

4. Open Discussion: Come together to share your observations after the reflection period. One partner speaks at a time while the other listens.
5. Identifying Common Ground: Highlight the patterns that both partners have identified. These are the critical patterns that need immediate attention.
6. Understanding Context: For each commonly identified pattern, discuss the circumstances under which they often occur. Are there specific triggers or situations?
7. Initial Steps for Change: Brainstorm some initial steps that can be taken to break these negative patterns.
8. Wrap-Up: Summarize the key points of the discussion and agree on one or two action items to work on before the next exercise session.

Additional Tips
- Be honest but gentle in your discussions. The goal is understanding, not blaming.
- Repeating this exercise at different stages of your relationship might be beneficial to track progress and make adjustments.

Follow-Up
After a week of implementing the agreed-upon changes, discuss the improvements, challenges, and any new insights.

Exercise: The 'Hot Button' Exercise

Introduction
Triggers can unexpectedly ignite negative interaction patterns, disrupting the harmony of a relationship. The 'Hot Button' Exercise allows couples to identify and understand these triggers, thereby equipping them with strategies to avoid falling into negative patterns.

Objective
The main goal of this exercise is to help couples become aware of specific triggers that often escalate conflicts or lead to negative interaction patterns. The exercise aims to discuss strategies to manage these triggers effectively.

Time Required
Approximately 20-30 minutes

Materials Needed
- Pen and paper for each participant
- A comfortable and private space for discussion

Instructions
1. Preparation: Make sure both partners are in a comfortable space where they won't be disturbed. Each partner should have a pen and paper.
2. Introductory Discussion: Start by acknowledging that everyone has triggers that can lead to negative patterns. Emphasize the importance of recognizing these to improve the relationship.
3. Individual Reflection: Give each partner 5-10 minutes to write down specific triggers they believe lead to negative patterns in their relationship.
4. Sharing and Discussion: Come back together and share your identified triggers. Make sure both partners actively listen and ask questions for clarity.
5. Strategy Brainstorming: Discuss potential strategies or coping mechanisms that could be employed to avoid these triggers. Write these down.
6. Action Plan: Agree on at least one strategy for each trigger to implement over the next week.
7. Wrap-Up: Conclude the exercise by summarizing the key points and reiterating the importance of being mindful of these triggers in day-to-day interactions.

Additional Tips
- This exercise can be emotional; approach it with sensitivity and openness.
- Avoid blaming language; focus on how you can support each other in avoiding triggers.

Follow-Up
After a week, reconvene to discuss how effective the strategies have been. Make adjustments as needed and commend each other for the progress made.

Exercise: Role-Reversal Scenario

Introduction

Empathy is a cornerstone of effective communication and conflict resolution in relationships. The 'Role-Reversal Scenario' exercise offers couples a unique opportunity to step into each other's shoes by role-playing a recent conflict, but with roles reversed.

Objective

The primary aim of this exercise is to deepen each partner's understanding of the other's thoughts, feelings, and reactions during conflicts. By experiencing a conflict from the other's viewpoint, couples can develop greater empathy and insight.

Time Required

Approximately 30-45 minutes

Materials Needed

- A quiet, comfortable space
- A list of recent conflicts or disagreements to choose from
- Note-taking materials (optional)

Instructions

1. . Preparation: Sit together in a quiet and comfortable setting where you won't be disturbed.
2. Conflict Selection: Each partner should consider a recent conflict that led to a disagreement or emotional reaction. Select one for the exercise.
3. Understanding the Original Roles: Briefly discuss the selected conflict, ensuring both partners remember the key points and emotions involved.
4. Role Reversal: Swap roles. Each partner should now assume the role of the other during the selected conflict.
5. Role-Playing: Act out the conflict with reversed roles. Aim to replicate the words, emotions, and reactions as best as you can.
6. Discussion: After the role-play, discuss the experience. What new insights have you gained about your partner's feelings and viewpoints?

7. Action Steps: Based on these new insights, identify specific behaviors or patterns that could be changed in future conflicts.
8. Wrap-Up: Summarize the main takeaways and agree on the next steps for implementing these insights into real-life conflicts.

Additional Tips
- Keep an open mind and avoid being defensive; the goal is to understand, not judge.
- If the exercise becomes too emotionally charged, it's okay to take a break and revisit it later.

Follow-Up
After a week of applying the new insights into real conflicts, regroup to discuss the effectiveness and any new observations.

Exercise: Pattern Interrupters

Introduction
Conflicts can escalate quickly, often following a predictable pattern of interaction. The use of 'Pattern Interrupters'—specific phrases or actions—can help disrupt this negative cycle. This exercise guides couples to create a list of pattern interrupters that can be employed during conflicts.

Objective
This exercise aims to identify and agree upon specific phrases or actions that can serve as 'interrupters' to stop the escalation of conflicts.

Time Required
Approximately 20-30 minutes

Materials Needed
- Note-taking materials
- A comfortable and private space for discussion

Instructions

1. Preparation: Sit together in a comfortable and quiet setting. Have your note-taking materials ready.
2. Brainstorming: Independently write down phrases or actions that could serve as pattern interrupters during conflicts.
3. Sharing: Share your list with your partner and discuss the feasibility and effectiveness of each item.
4. Agreement: Agree upon a set of pattern interrupters you are comfortable using.
5. Practice: Role-play a hypothetical conflict scenario and practice using the agreed-upon pattern interrupters.
6. Wrap-Up: Summarize the interrupters you've agreed upon and commit to using them in real-life conflicts.

Additional Tips

- The phrases or actions should be easy to remember and quick to use.
- They should be neutral or positive to avoid further escalation.

Follow-Up

After using the agreed-upon pattern interrupters in real-life scenarios, regroup to discuss their effectiveness and make any necessary adjustments.

Exercise: Action-Reaction Mapping

Introduction

Relationship conflicts often escalate through a series of actions and reactions from both parties. Understanding this dynamic can provide valuable insights for de-escalation and problem-solving. The 'Action-Reaction Mapping' exercise aims to help couples dissect a recent conflict and identify the key actions and reactions that led to escalation.

Objective

The primary objective of this exercise is to analyze a recent conflict in terms of actions and reactions from both partners. This will help understand how conflicts escalate and identify ways to manage them better.

Time Required
Approximately 40-60 minutes

Materials Needed
- A large sheet of paper or a whiteboard
- Markers or pens
- A comfortable and private space for discussion

Instructions
1. Preparation: Sit together in a comfortable private setting with the paper and markers ready.
2. Conflict Selection: Choose a recent conflict that both of you remember well.
3. Initial Mapping: On the paper, create a timeline of the conflict—Mark down the key actions and reactions from both sides that escalated the situation.
4. Discussion: Discuss each action and reaction on the timeline. Try to understand the emotions and thoughts that led to each.
5. Identify Triggers: Highlight any actions or reactions that trigger further escalation.
6. Potential Solutions: Discuss alternative actions or reactions that could have de-escalated the situation.
7. Summary: Summarize the key insights gained from this exercise.
8. Action Plan: Decide specific strategies to avoid triggers and de-escalate future conflicts.
9. Wrap-Up: Conclude by acknowledging the effort and openness from both sides and agree to apply the learned strategies in future conflicts.

Additional Tips
- Be as objective as possible while mapping the actions and reactions.
- Avoid blaming or criticizing; the focus is on understanding the dynamics.

Follow-Up
After applying the new strategies in real-life conflicts, meet again to discuss their effectiveness and make it necessary.

Exercise: The Repair Attempt

Introduction

Even the best of relationships can encounter conflicts that follow a negative pattern. The ability to recognize these patterns and make 'repair attempts' is crucial for relationship health. This exercise focuses on teaching couples how to make and practice repair attempts.

Objective

This exercise aims to teach couples how to make 'repair attempts'—conscious efforts to de-escalate conflict—when they notice a negative pattern forming and to practice implementing these attempts.

Time Required

Approximately 30-45 minutes

Materials Needed

- Note-taking materials
- A comfortable and private space for discussion

Instructions

1. Preparation: Sit together in a comfortable and quiet setting. Have your note-taking materials ready.
2. Identify Patterns: Discuss recent conflicts to identify recurring negative patterns.
3. Brainstorm Repair Attempts: Both partners should brainstorm phrases or actions that could serve as repair attempts during conflicts.
4. Discuss: Share your suggestions and discuss the feasibility and effectiveness of each.
5. Agreement: Agree upon a set of repair attempts that both of you are comfortable using.
6. Practice: Role-play a hypothetical conflict scenario and practice implementing the agreed-upon repair attempts.
7. Wrap-Up: Summarize the repair attempts you've agreed upon and commit to using them in real-life conflicts.

Additional Tips
- Repair attempts should be simple, direct, and easy to remember.
- They should convey sincerity and a genuine desire to resolve the conflict.

Follow-Up
After using the agreed-upon repair attempts in real-life scenarios, meet again to discuss their effectiveness and make any necessary adjustments.

Exercise: Your Conflict Style

Introduction
Understanding how each partner approaches conflict can provide invaluable insights into the dynamics of your relationship. The 'Your Conflict Style' exercise includes a quiz identifying each partner's predominant conflict style, such as 'avoidant' or 'confrontational.'

Objective
This exercise aims to help couples identify their individual conflict styles and discuss how these styles may contribute to negative interaction patterns within the relationship.

Time Required
Approximately 45 minutes

Materials Needed
- Printed or digital copies of the Conflict Style Quiz
- Pen and paper for note-taking
- A comfortable and private space for discussion

Instructions
1. Preparation: Make sure you are in a quiet and comfortable space where you won't be disturbed. Have the quiz and note-taking materials ready.
2. Taking the Quiz: Each partner takes the Conflict Style Quiz independently.
3. Scoring the Quiz: After both partners have completed the quiz, score your answers to identify your predominant conflict style.

4. Discussion: Share your results. Discuss what you've learned about your conflict styles and how they might contribute to negative patterns in your relationship.
5. Action Steps: Discuss how you can adapt your conflict styles to be more constructive or better accommodate each other's styles.
6. Wrap-Up: Summarize the insights gained and agree on the next steps for applying this new understanding to real-world conflicts.

The Conflict Style Quiz
Questions

1. I tend to avoid discussing the issue and hope it will disappear.
*   - Never (1)
*   - Rarely (2)
*   - Sometimes (3)
*   - Often (4)
*   - Always (5)

2. I try to confront the issue directly and solve the problem.
*   - Never (1)
*   - Rarely (2)
*   - Sometimes (3)
*   - Often (4)
*   - Always (5)

3. I become defensive and start making excuses.
*   - Never (1)
*   - Rarely (2)
*   - Sometimes (3)
*   - Often (4)
*   - Always (5)

4. I seek compromise to resolve the issue.
*   - Never (1)
*   - Rarely (2)
*   - Sometimes (3)
*   - Often (4)
*   - Always (5)

5. I shut down emotionally and withdraw from the situation.
- - Never (1)
- - Rarely (2)
- - Sometimes (3)
- - Often (4)
- - Always (5)

6. I try to understand my partner's point of view.
- - Never (1)
- - Rarely (2)
- - Sometimes (3)
- - Often (4)
- - Always (5)

7. I raise my voice or become aggressive.
- - Never (1)
- - Rarely (2)
- - Sometimes (3)
- - Often (4)
- - Always (5)

8. I tend to blame my partner for the issue.
- - Never (1)
- - Rarely (2)
- - Sometimes (3)
- - Often (4)
- - Always (5)

9. I avoid conflict by agreeing even when I don't really agree.
- - Never (1)
- - Rarely (2)
- - Sometimes (3)
- - Often (4)
- - Always (5)

10. I try to change the subject to avoid confrontation.
- - Never (1)

- - Rarely (2)
- - Sometimes (3)
- - Often (4)
- - Always (5)

11. I listen carefully and ask questions to clarify the issue.
- - Never (1)
- - Rarely (2)
- - Sometimes (3)
- - Often (4)
- - Always (5)

12. I become sarcastic or use humor to deflect the issue.
- - Never (1)
- - Rarely (2)
- - Sometimes (3)
- - Often (4)
- - Always (5)

13. I admit my mistakes and try to make amends.
- - Never (1)
- - Rarely (2)
- - Sometimes (3)
- - Often (4)
- - Always (5)

14. I feel overwhelmed and shut down during conflicts.
- - Never (1)
- - Rarely (2)
- - Sometimes (3)
- - Often (4)
- - Always (5)

15. I ask for time to think before discussing the issue further.
- - Never (1)
- - Rarely (2)
- - Sometimes (3)

- - Often (4)
- - Always (5)

16. I bring up past issues to strengthen my argument.
- - Never (1)
- - Rarely (2)
- - Sometimes (3)
- - Often (4)
- - Always (5)

17. I try to see the bigger picture without getting caught up in details.
- - Never (1)
- - Rarely (2)
- - Sometimes (3)
- - Often (4)
- - Always (5)

18. I get anxious and find it hard to express myself.
- - Never (1)
- - Rarely (2)
- - Sometimes (3)
- - Often (4)
- - Always (5)

19. I try to resolve the issue as quickly as possible, even if it means compromising.
- - Never (1)
- - Rarely (2)
- - Sometimes (3)
- - Often (4)
- - Always (5)

20. I tend to give the silent treatment when upset.
- - Never (1)
- - Rarely (2)
- - Sometimes (3)
- - Often (4)
- - Always (5)

Scoring Key
- Avoidant: High scores on questions 1, 5, 9, 10, 14, 20
- Confrontational: High scores on questions 2, 7, 8, 12, 16
- Problem-Solver: High scores on questions 4, 6, 11, 13, 17, 19
- Insecure: High scores on questions 3, 15, 18

To find your predominant style, calculate the total scores for each category. The category with the highest total score is your predominant conflict style.

Additional Tips
- Be honest in your responses to get the most accurate results.
- Keep an open mind during the discussion, focusing on understanding rather than judging.

Follow-Up
Revisit the exercise after a month to assess any changes in your conflict styles and the impact on your relationship dynamics.

Exercise: The 'What If' Game

Introduction
Conflicts in relationships are sometimes predictable, stemming from recurring issues or situations. The 'What If' Game allows couples to discuss hypothetical scenarios commonly leading to conflict proactively. Couples can be better prepared for future situations by brainstorming better ways to handle them.

Objective
This exercise aims to engage in a constructive dialogue about potential future conflicts. This proactive approach helps couples to explore alternative ways of handling tricky scenarios.

Time Required
Approximately 30-45 minutes

Materials Needed
- A list of hypothetical scenarios that often lead to conflict
- Note-taking materials (optional)
- A comfortable and private space for discussion

Instructions
1. Preparation: Sit together in a comfortable and quiet setting. Have your list of hypothetical scenarios and note-taking materials ready.
2. Scenario Selection: One partner picks a hypothetical scenario from the list.
3. Initial Discussion: Discuss your usual reactions and outcomes to this scenario.
4. Brainstorming: Both partners brainstorm alternative ways to handle the situation to avoid conflict.
5. Agreement: Agree on one or more strategies to use in a real-world instance of this scenario.
6. Repeat: Repeat steps 2-5 for different scenarios.
7. Wrap-Up: Summarize the agreed-upon strategies and commit to trying them in real-life situations.

Additional Tips
- Try to be as realistic as possible in your brainstorming.
- Keep an open mind and be willing to compromise.

Follow-Up
After trying the agreed-upon strategies in real-life scenarios, come back to discuss their effectiveness and make any necessary adjustments.

WEEK 4

Enhancing Emotional Connection

Welcome to a transformative journey—a journey that will take you deep into the heart of your relationship to explore, understand, and ultimately enhance the emotional connection you share with your partner. Ah, emotional connection, the soul food that nourishes relationships! The invisible thread binds two people, the secret sauce that makes good relationships great. But what happens when that thread begins to fray or, worse, snaps? That's precisely what this workbook aims to address.

Before diving into the nuances of emotional connection, let's clear what it is not. It's not just about romantic dinners, surprise gifts, or physical intimacy. While these elements can supplement an emotional connection, they don't define it. Emotional connection is the invisible bond that goes beyond the surface, delving deep into the emotional landscape that each partner brings to the relationship. It's about truly 'seeing' each other—flaws, vulnerabilities, dreams, etc.

So why focus on enhancing emotional connection? Because it's the bedrock on which all other relationship aspects are built—communication, trust, intimacy, and even conflict resolution. Think of your relationship as a magnificent skyscraper. Emotional connection is its foundation, ensuring that the structure can withstand the storms and stresses of life. A weak foundation makes a shaky building susceptible to cracks and, eventually, collapse.

This workbook is designed as a comprehensive guide to help you navigate the complex terrains of emotional connection. Whether you're experiencing emotional distance, struggling with attachment issues, or simply looking to strengthen the existing emotional bond, we've got you covered. We'll explore a variety of topics, such as emotional attunement, the effects of prolonged emotional distance, coping strategies, and much more. Each section is designed to offer insights, actionable advice, and exercises to help you and your partner foster a deeper emotional connection.

We invite you to dive deep, be vulnerable, and engage with this workbook wholeheartedly. After all, it's not just about reading; it's about doing, feeling, and experiencing.

Emotional Attunement

Emotional attunement is often likened to a dance, a harmonious interplay between two individuals where each is attuned to the emotional cues and needs of the other. Imagine a pair of dancers gliding across the floor momentarily, so in sync that it's hard to tell where one ends and the other begins. That's emotional attunement, in a nutshell, a level of understanding and responsiveness that elevates any relationship to a state of harmony.

What is Emotional Attunement?

Emotional attunement goes beyond mere understanding; it's an intuitive sense of your partner's feelings, sometimes even before they articulate them. This isn't mind-reading or a magical sixth sense; it's a cultivated skill that comes from being emotionally present and observant. It's about picking up on subtle cues—a look, a sigh, a tone of voice—and responding in a way that makes your partner feel seen, heard, and understood.

Lack of Emotional Attunement

When emotional attunement is missing, the impact can be jarring. The dance becomes a clumsy shuffle, leading to frequent missteps and collisions. A lack of emotional attunement manifests as a disconnect, where each partner feels like they are navigating the emotional terrain alone. The signals get mixed, the cues are missed, and the result is often an escalating cycle of misunderstandings and hurt feelings.

Signs of Emotional Distance

So, how can you tell if your relationship is suffering from a lack of emotional attunement? Some signs are obvious—arguments that erupt out of nowhere, a feeling of walking on eggshells around each other, or a decline in physical intimacy. Others may be subtler, such as a reluctance to share feelings or a general sense of emotional flatness.

Difficulties in Establishing or Sustaining Relationships

The lack of emotional attunement can also extend beyond the relationship, affecting your ability to form and sustain connections with others. After all, if you're struggling to tune into the emotional frequency of someone as close to you as a partner, it's likely that the ripple effects will be felt in other interpersonal interactions as well.

Difficulties in Showing Love or Compassion

Emotional attunement isn't just about understanding; it's also about response. A lack of attunement can lead to difficulties expressing love, affection, or compassion in ways that resonate with your partner. It's like speaking different emotional languages, where the message gets lost in translation.

Building Emotional Attunement

Building emotional attunement is akin to cultivating a garden. It requires time, effort, and a deep understanding of the unique 'emotional soil' you and your partner bring to the relationship. Yes, it's a labor of love, but the fruits of this labor are deeply fulfilling. So, let's roll up our sleeves and dig in, shall we?

Validate Their Emotions

Emotional validation is a powerful tool in building attunement. It's about acknowledging your partner's feelings without judgment. You don't have to agree with them; you must make them feel heard. This creates a safe emotional space, encouraging open and honest communication.

Avoid Judgment

Judgment is the arch-enemy of emotional attunement. Think of it as the 'weed' in your emotional garden, one that can quickly choke the life out of empathy and understanding. Avoiding judgment isn't about turning a blind eye to issues; it's about approaching them with an open mind and heart.

Find Common Ground

Finding common ground is like planting 'companion plants' in your emotional garden—those that naturally grow well together. Shared values, interests, or even shared struggles can serve as this common ground, reinforcing the emotional bond.

Be Present

Emotional attunement requires presence, both physical and emotional. It's about being 'there,' not just as a physical entity but as an emotional support. Think of this as the 'sunlight' your emotional garden needs—consistent, warm, and life-giving.

The Role of Empathy

Empathy is the 'fertilizer' in this analogy; it enriches emotional understanding. It allows you to step into your partner's shoes, offering insights that intellectual understanding can't. Cultivating empathy often involves active listening and open-ended questioning, which pave the way for deeper emotional attunement.

Emotional Cues and Their Importance

Being attuned to your partner's emotional cues—be it a sigh, a certain look, or even a tone of voice—is akin to understanding the 'signs' your garden shows when it needs water or is ready for harvest. These cues offer a wealth of information, often acting as gateways to deeper emotional states.

The Power of Emotional Language

Building emotional attunement also involves learning each other's 'emotional language.' This goes beyond words to include gestures, expressions, and even silences. Once you become fluent in this language, emotional connection becomes a natural, effortless flow.

Effects of Prolonged Emotional Distance

Emotional distance isn't always glaringly obvious. Sometimes, it creeps in subtly, masquerading as routine or 'normalcy.' But like a slow leak in a tire, it gradually deflates the relationship until what's left is a flat, lifeless partnership. This chapter aims to spotlight the often-underestimated consequences of prolonged emotional distance and why it's crucial to address it.

Social Isolation

One of the most immediate effects of emotional distance is social isolation. You might be sitting beside each other, but it feels miles apart emotionally. This kind of isolation doesn't just strain the relationship; it often trickles into your social life, complicating interactions with friends and family.

Negative Self-Perception

A prolonged emotional disconnect can lead to negative self-perception. You may start doubting your worth, questioning your attractiveness, or even your capability to be in a relationship. This erodes self-esteem and can have a long-lasting impact on your mental health.

Reduced Sense of Purpose

When emotional connection is strong, it often infuses a sense of purpose into the relationship. Each partner feels like they are a part of something greater than themselves. Emotional distance erodes this, making the relationship feel less like a partnership and more like cohabitation without a cause.

Emotional Exhaustion

Maintaining a facade of 'normalcy' in the face of emotional distance is draining. It's like running a marathon with no finish line in sight. This emotional exhaustion isn't just mentally taxing; it can manifest physically, leading to symptoms like fatigue, insomnia, or even chronic health issues.

The Domino Effect on Mental Health

The strain of emotional distance often acts as a precursor to mental health issues like anxiety and depression. It's a vicious cycle—the more anxious or depressed you feel, the harder it is to bridge the emotional gap, perpetuating the cycle of distance and mental health decline.

Impact on Physical Intimacy

It's no secret that emotional and physical intimacy are closely linked. Prolonged emotional distance often leads to a decline in physical intimacy, exacerbating the emotional disconnect—a double whammy that puts the relationship in a precarious position.

The Ripple Effect on Other Relationships

Emotional distance in a romantic relationship often has a ripple effect, affecting your relationships with friends, family, and even colleagues. It's like an emotional cold front that chills your romantic partnership and interpersonal climate.

Coping with Detachment

So, you've identified that emotional distance has crept into your relationship. The next question is, what can you do about it? Coping with emotional detachment isn't about quick fixes or Band-Aid solutions but sustainable, meaningful changes. Let's delve into some ways you can navigate this emotional maze.

Identify the Cause
The first step in coping with detachment is to understand its root cause. Is it a recent event that has created a rift, or is it a gradual buildup of unresolved issues? Identifying the cause helps you decide the best course of action, like diagnosing an ailment before prescribing medication.

Seek Professional Help
Sometimes, the emotional divide can be so vast that you may need a mediator to bridge the gap. This is where professional help comes in. Whether it's couples therapy or individual counseling, professional guidance can offer invaluable insights and coping strategies.

Practice Mindfulness
Mindfulness is the art of being present and plays a critical role in coping with emotional detachment. By being mindful, you become more attuned to your emotional state and that of your partner, paving the way for improved communication and emotional connection.

Engage in Self-Care
Emotional detachment can be draining, both mentally and physically. Self-care isn't just about pampering yourself; it's about rejuvenating your emotional well-being and giving you the strength to face relationship challenges head-on.

Connect with Others
While focusing on mending the emotional detachment in your romantic relationship, don't underestimate the power of a strong support network. Friends and family can offer a different perspective, emotional support, or even a listening ear when things get tough.

Avoid Self-Medicating with Substances
It's tempting to seek refuge in substances like alcohol or drugs when dealing with emotional pain. However, this slippery slope often exacerbates the problem, creating additional issues to deal with.

Writing as a Form of Therapy
The written word can be a powerful tool in coping with emotional detachment. Whether journaling your thoughts, writing letters you may never send, or even engaging in creative writing, putting pen to paper can be therapeutic.

Getting a New Perspective
Sometimes, a change of scenery or even a change in routine can offer a new perspective on an old problem. It's like stepping back from a painting to see the whole picture. A fresh viewpoint can offer new ways to approach emotional detachment.

Allowing Vulnerability
Vulnerability is often seen as a weakness, but in the context of emotional detachment, it's a strength. Allowing yourself to be vulnerable can open doors to deeper emotional connection, breaking down walls built up over time.

Coping with detachment is a journey that requires patience, effort, and a lot of emotional intelligence. The following chapters will dive deeper into attachment bonds, emotional intimacy, and more. For now, let this chapter serve as your roadmap for navigating the rocky terrains of emotional detachment.

Allowing Vulnerability and Attachment Bonds

When you hear the word 'vulnerability,' what comes to mind? For many, it evokes a sense of weakness or exposure. But in the context of a romantic relationship, vulnerability is the cornerstone of emotional intimacy. It transforms a relationship from a mere association into an emotional refuge. This chapter will explore the concept of vulnerability and its closely related cousin—attachment bonds.

Allowing Vulnerability
Vulnerability is the emotional equivalent of an open door. It invites your partner into your internal world, offering them a glimpse into your fears, hopes, and dreams. But more than that, it's a mutual exchange—a two-way street where both partners share and receive. So, why is it so hard for us to be vulnerable? Often, it's the fear of judgment or rejection. But the irony is that vulnerability deepens emotional bonds and fosters trust.

Attachment Bonds
Attachment bonds are the invisible threads that connect us to our loved ones. The safety nets catch us when we fall, offering emotional security and stability. These bonds are often formed in early childhood but play a significant role in our adult relationships. They are the bedrock upon which emotional intimacy is built.

Effects of Insecure Attachment

Not all attachment bonds are created equal. Insecure attachments can lead to a host of relationship issues, from fear of abandonment to emotional volatility. It's like building a house on a shaky foundation; no matter how beautiful it looks, it's always at risk of collapsing.

Fear of Rejection

One of the most common manifestations of insecure attachment is the fear of rejection. This often stems from past experiences where vulnerability was met with disdain or dismissal. It acts as an emotional barrier, preventing true intimacy.

Need for Constant Reassurance

Insecure attachment often manifests as a constant need for reassurance. It's like an emotional itch that never quite goes away, leading to behaviors like excessive texting or clinginess. While reassurance is a natural part of any relationship, the 'constant' need for it can be draining for both partners.

Jealousy and Possessiveness

Insecure attachment can also fuel feelings of jealousy and possessiveness. This corrosive emotion can eat away at a relationship's trust and mutual respect. It's essential to address the root causes of such feelings to foster a healthy emotional bond.

Fear of Abandonment

The fear of abandonment is another red flag of insecure attachment. It can lead to self-sabotaging behaviors, as the person preemptively distances themselves to avoid the pain of being left. This creates a self-fulfilling prophecy, where the fear of abandonment leads to actions that make it more likely.

Building Secure Relationship Attachments

So, how do you build secure relationship attachments? The key lies in fostering open communication, mutual respect, and emotional transparency. It involves active listening, empathic understanding, and, most importantly, the courage to be vulnerable.

Building Emotional Intimacy through Shared Experience

If emotional intimacy were a house, shared experiences would be bricks and mortar. The collective memories, private jokes, and mutual triumphs and failures turn a relationship from a contractual agreement into an emotional sanctuary. This chapter will explore how to cultivate emotional intimacy through shared experiences.

The Importance of Shared Experiences

Shared experiences are the lifeblood of emotional intimacy. They provide a common ground, a mutual history that deepens the emotional bond between partners. They turn 'you and me' into 'us,' creating a collective identity greater than the sum of its parts.

The Joy of Simple Moments

When discussing shared experiences, thinking of grand gestures or bucket-list adventures is easy. While those are wonderful, the simple, mundane moments often hold the most emotional weight. The silent comfort of a shared sunset, the unspoken understanding in a glance, or even the mutual laughter over an inside joke are threads that weave the fabric of emotional intimacy.

The Role of Conflict

It may sound counterintuitive, but conflict plays a significant role in building emotional intimacy. How you handle disagreements, make up, and navigate the choppy waters of conflict says a lot about your emotional connection's health. In the furnace of conflict, the metal of your relationship is truly tested.

The Power of Vulnerability in Shared Experiences

The willingness to be vulnerable in shared experiences can exponentially increase their emotional impact. Whether opening up about your fears during a late-night conversation or showing your true self, warts and all, vulnerability elevates a shared experience from a 'moment' to a 'memory.'

Quality Time vs. Quantity Time

In the digital age, where distractions are aplenty, the quality of shared time becomes more important than the quantity. It's not about how much time you spend together, but how 'present' you are in those moments. Quality time is an investment in your emotional intimacy bank.

The Role of Empathy

Empathy is the silent partner in the dance of emotional intimacy. It allows you to step into your partner's shoes, feel their joy or pain, and share experiences on a deeper emotional level. Cultivating empathy is akin to tending a garden; it requires care, attention, and much love.

Navigating the Emotional Landscape

Building emotional intimacy is like navigating an ever-changing landscape. It requires adaptability, the willingness to evolve, and the courage to venture into uncharted emotional territories. Every shared experience adds a layer to this landscape, enriching it with new textures and colors.

Emotional intimacy is not a destination but a journey that requires mutual effort, a sense of adventure, and an open heart. In the upcoming chapters, we will explore more specific strategies for nurturing emotional intimacy and maintaining a strong emotional connection. But for now, let this chapter be your guidebook for building an emotionally rich and rewarding relationship.

Your Personalized Workbook

While this workbook offers a structured approach, it's designed to be flexible. The exercises provided don't have to be taken in the order they are listed. Feel free to pick and choose exercises that resonate with you and are most appropriate for the specific challenges or circumstances you're facing. Consider this workbook as a menu of options, not a set sequence of steps.

Chapter Exercises

Exercise: Active Listening Practice

Introduction

Active listening is a cornerstone of emotional connection and effective communication. This exercise aims to practice the skill of active listening between couples, reinforcing emotional intimacy.

Objective

This exercise aims to practice active listening skills where one partner speaks about their day or a specific issue, and the other listens actively, reflecting on what they have heard.

Time Required

Approximately 20-30 minutes

Materials Needed

- A quiet and comfortable space for discussion
- A timer (optional)

Instructions

1. Preparation: Choose a quiet and comfortable setting where you both can talk without distractions. Set a timer for 10 minutes per person if desired.
2. Speaking Turn: One partner starts by discussing their day or a specific issue they want to discuss.
3. Active Listening: The other partner listens attentively without interrupting or offering advice.
4. Reflection: After the speaker has finished, the listener reflects on what they have heard, summarizing the key points and emotions expressed.
5. Switch Roles: Swap roles and repeat steps 2-4.
6. Discussion: After both turns are complete, discuss the experience. What was it like to listen actively? What was it like to be listened to in this manner?

7. Wrap-Up: Summarize any insights gained from the exercise and commit to practicing active listening in daily interactions.

Additional Tips
- Try to maintain eye contact and show non-verbal signs of listening (nodding, etc.).
- The listener should resist the urge to formulate responses while the other is speaking.

Follow-Up
Incorporate active listening into your daily conversations and periodically check in with each other about how it's affecting your emotional connection.

Exercise: The 'No Advice' Session

Introduction
Sometimes, emotional support is more valuable than advice, especially when navigating complex emotions or situations. The 'No Advice' Session focuses on providing a space where couples can share problems while receiving emotional support only.

Objective
This exercise aims to practice offering emotional support without giving advice. This can deepen emotional connection and foster a safe emotional environment.

Time Required
Approximately 20-30 minutes

Materials Needed
- A quiet and comfortable space for discussion

Instructions
1. Preparation: Choose a quiet and comfortable setting where you both can talk without distractions.
2. Problem Sharing: One partner starts by sharing a problem or issue they are currently facing.

3. Emotional Support: The other partner listens and provides emotional support but refrains from offering advice.
4. Switch Roles: Swap roles and repeat steps 2-3.
5. Discussion: After both partners have had a turn, discuss the experience. How did it feel to offer only emotional support? How did it feel to receive it?
6. Wrap-Up: Summarize any insights gained from this exercise and discuss how to incorporate this approach into your relationship.

Additional Tips
- It may be challenging to refrain from giving advice; focus on empathetic listening instead.
- Use affirming language and non-verbal cues to show your support.

Follow-Up
Practice implementing this 'No Advice' approach when your partner seeks emotional support. Regularly check in to assess how it's impacting your emotional connection.

Exercise: The 'Why I Love You' List

Introduction
The power of love lies not just in actions but also in emotional qualities and the feelings they evoke. The 'Why I Love You' List exercise provides a platform for couples to express and explore these deeper emotional aspects.

Objective
This exercise aims for each partner to create a list of reasons why they love the other. The focus is not just on actions but also on emotional qualities. The lists are then shared and discussed.

Time Required
Approximately 20-30 minutes

Materials Needed
- Note-taking materials
- A quiet and comfortable space for discussion

Instructions
1. Preparation: Find a quiet and comfortable setting to focus without distractions. Have your note-taking materials ready.
2. Writing: Each partner takes 10 minutes to write down why they love the other, focusing on emotional qualities and actions.
3. Sharing: Take turns sharing your lists with each other.
4. Discussion: Discuss the lists, exploring the emotional qualities mentioned. How do they make you feel? Are there any surprises?
5. Wrap-Up: Reflect on the experience and discuss how to nurture these qualities and feelings in your daily life.

Additional Tips
- Be as specific as possible in your list to make it more meaningful.
- Keep the list where you can revisit it, especially during challenging times.

Follow-Up
Consider making this exercise a regular practice, perhaps on anniversaries or other significant dates, to keep the emotional connection fresh and meaningful.

Exercise: Open-Hearted Questions

Introduction
Probing emotional topics can deepen emotional intimacy and understanding. The Open-Hearted Questions exercise is designed to create a space for couples to explore these topics.

Objective
This exercise aims to create a list of open-ended questions designed to probe emotional topics. Couples will spend an evening answering these questions to deepen their emotional connection.

Time Required
Approximately 1-2 hours

Materials Needed
- Note-taking materials
- A quiet and comfortable space for discussion

Instructions
1. Preparation: Find a quiet and comfortable setting to talk without distractions.
2. Question Creation: Independently write 5-10 open-ended questions to probe emotional topics (e.g., 'What does love mean to you?').
3. Sharing and Merging: Share your lists and merge them to create one master list of questions.
4. Question Time: Take turns asking and answering questions from the master list.
5. Discussion: Discuss the experience, focusing on the emotions evoked by the questions and answers.
6. Wrap-Up: Reflect on any new insights or understandings from this exercise.

Additional Tips
- Be honest but considerate in your answers.
- If a question triggers a deeper topic, feel free to explore it more.

Follow-Up
Review your master list of questions periodically and consider adding new ones as your relationship evolves.

Exercise: The 'Best Self' Exercise

Introduction
Everyone has a 'best self'—a version of themselves where they feel most confident, happy, and fulfilled. The 'Best Self' Exercise explores what brings out this best self in each partner and how the other contributes to it.

Objective
This exercise aims to identify and discuss what brings out the 'best self' in you and explore how each partner contributes to bringing out that best self.

Time Required
Approximately 30-45 minutes

Materials Needed
- Note-taking materials
- A quiet and comfortable space for discussion

Instructions
1. Preparation: Find a quiet and comfortable setting to talk without distractions.
2. Best Self Identification: Individually think about situations or conditions where you feel like your 'best self.'
3. Sharing: Take turns sharing your thoughts about your 'best self.'
4. Contribution Discussion: Discuss how you contribute to bringing out the other's 'best self.'
5. Insights and Actions: Identify actionable steps you can take to help each other be your 'best selves' more often.
6. Wrap-Up: Summarize the key takeaways from the exercise and commit to implementing the actionable steps.

Additional Tips
- Keep an open mind and heart during the discussion.
- This exercise can be emotional; handle the conversation with care and sensitivity.

Follow-Up
Regularly check in to assess how you are doing in bringing out each other's 'best selves.'

Resolving Conflicts

Acknowledging that conflict is a part of relationships and needs a resolution is half the battle won. It's as inevitable in a relationship as forgetting to take out the trash or arguing about where to eat for dinner. If you haven't had a heated debate over the virtues of sushi over pizza, are you even in a relationship?

But let's get serious for a moment. Conflict isn't just those little spats over Netflix choices or whose turn to do the dishes. It can escalate, affecting not just your relationship but your emotional well-being and even your health. And that's why you're here: to explore, understand, and ultimately become a master of resolving conflicts. You're not just saving your relationship; you're also investing in your mental peace. It's the kind of two-for-one deal that's better than any Black Friday sale.

This workbook is designed as your guide and confidant. Think of it as that wise old sage you seek when you're lost—except it's made of paper and has no long, flowing beard. Throughout these pages, we'll delve into the intricacies of why conflicts happen, how they affect you, and most importantly, how to resolve them in a way that leaves your relationship stronger and more resilient. Don't worry; you won't be going at it alone. I'll be right here, guiding you through real-life scenario exercises and maybe even making you laugh a little because, let's face it, a spoonful of humor makes personal growth go down easier.

So, buckle up! You're about to embark on a transformative journey to becoming the best version of yourself in your relationship. By the end of this workbook, you won't just be resolving conflicts; you'll be navigating through them like a seasoned sailor through the high seas, steering your relationship toward the serene shores of mutual understanding and respect.

The Importance of Conflict Resolution in Sustaining a Healthy Relationship

Imagine standing in front of a beautiful, intricate tapestry. From afar, it looks harmonious and well-balanced, but as you get closer, you notice that some threads are frayed and even a few holes. Much like that tapestry, relationships appear different depending on how closely you look. The tapestry of your relationship is woven from many threads—love, trust, friendship, and yes, conflict. Conflict is not the aberration in an otherwise smooth relationship; it's an integral part. It's one of those threads that give the relationship its texture, its dynamism, and its depth.

Here's the kicker: ignoring the frayed threads and the holes won't make them disappear. Likewise, avoiding conflicts in your relationship won't make the issues disappear. They'll fester, undermining the strength and beauty of your relational tapestry over time. You wouldn't ignore a leaky roof or a rattling engine, would you? Then why treat the emotional architecture of your relationship any differently?

Conflict resolution is the cornerstone upon which the edifice of trust is built in a relationship. Every time you successfully navigate a disagreement, you're essentially laying another brick in the wall of trust between you and your partner. Trust isn't just about fidelity or keeping promises; it's also about knowing that your emotional well-being is safe with another person. And there's nothing that reassures this more than coming out of a conflict with a sense of resolution, understanding, and mutual growth.

Resolving conflicts teaches much about your partner and yourself—your triggers, emotional safe spaces, and non-negotiables. This self-awareness and mutual understanding breed emotional resilience, a quality that helps you bounce back from future conflicts even stronger than before. Moreover, a special kind of intimacy comes from resolving conflicts. It's an intimacy born from vulnerability, from showing your partner your true self—warts, fears, and all—and being accepted and loved regardless.

The impact of unresolved conflict isn't just emotional; it's psychological. Continuous conflict without resolution can lead to stress, which in turn can manifest as physical symptoms, including headaches, digestive issues, and sleep problems. Who knew that the path from your argument about doing the dishes to your insomnia was a straight line? Effective conflict resolution can be a relief valve for this stress, offering not just emotional but also physical well-being.

Finally, let's not forget that conflict often arises from change, which is the only constant in life. Whether moving cities, changing jobs, or growing a family, life events will throw your relationship into flux. Conflict resolution is how you adjust the sails of your relationship to navigate these changing winds. The dynamic equilibrium keeps your relationship stable yet flexible, like a skyscraper swaying subtly in the wind.

In essence, conflict resolution is not just about solving a problem; it's about strengthening the relationship and preparing it for future challenges. It's about ensuring that the tapestry of your relationship remains strong, beautiful, and vibrant, no matter how closely you look.

Benefits of Effective Conflict Resolution

Trust is the bedrock of any successful relationship, and effective conflict resolution acts like the mason who carefully lays each stone. Every time you successfully resolve a conflict, you're not just finding a solution to a problem; you're building trust, brick by brick. It's like a bank where you make emotional deposits. The more successful resolutions you have, the greater your trust savings. This accumulated trust becomes your safety net for future conflicts and disagreements. Imagine being able to disagree without fearing that the relationship might crumble—that's the power of increased trust. It acts as both a cushion and a catalyst, softening the blows of future conflicts and accelerating your journey toward resolution.

Empathy is the ability to understand and share another person's feelings, and it grows exponentially when conflicts are resolved effectively. Think of it as a window into your partner's world. The more windows you have, the more light shines through, illuminating the dark corners of misunderstanding and assumptions. But empathy is not a one-way street; it's a bustling highway of mutual emotional exchange. As you navigate through conflicts, you learn the language of your partner's emotions—their fears, joys, triggers, and safe spaces. This mutual understanding is a treasure trove that enriches your relationship, making it more nuanced and layered.

Conflict resolution is relationship algebra. The more problems you solve, the better you get at it. But unlike algebra, there's no dreaded x to solve for; instead, you learn to balance the equation of your relationship. You develop a knack for identifying issues before they escalate into major conflicts. It's like having a sixth sense for relationship well-being. Over time, this skill extends beyond the relationship into other areas of your life. Whether negotiating a raise at work or planning a family holiday, your honed problem-solving skills will stand you in good stead.

Respect is the quiet hero in the narrative of conflict resolution. It's the underlying tone in all communications, the pause before you react, and the restraint when you disagree. As you successfully navigate conflicts, respect grows in the fertile ground prepared by trust, empathy, and effective communication. Greater respect means giving your partner the space to be themselves, accepting them as they are, and acknowledging that their viewpoints are as valid as yours, even if you disagree. In a relationship steeped in mutual respect, conflicts lose their antagonistic edge and become growth opportunities.

Imagine a home. Not just a house with walls and a roof but a home where you feel utterly safe and secure. That's what emotional safety feels like in a relationship. Effective conflict resolution establishes this sanctuary. Knowing that conflicts can be resolved without damaging the relationship provides a sense of emotional safety that is both liberating and empowering. It's like wearing a parachute; you're more willing to take the leap, secure in the knowledge that you're safe even if you fall. Emotional safety transforms the very fabric of your relationship, making it a nurturing environment where love, understanding, and mutual respect can flourish.

The Costs of Avoiding Conflict Resolution

Short-Term vs Long-Term Impact

In the heat of the moment, avoiding conflict might seem like the easy way out. It's the quick fix, the temporary Band-Aid that stops the bleeding but doesn't heal the wound. Short-term, it can feel like a win; you avoid a heated argument, maintain a surface-level peace, and life seemingly goes on as usual. But here's the rub: avoiding conflict is essentially a loan taken out against your relationship's future.Just like financial debt accumulates interest, emotional debt accrues over time in the form of unresolved issues and bottled-up feelings. In the long term, this debt can become overwhelming, reaching a tipping point where the relationship can neither bear the weight nor pay off the emotional debt. Essentially, what starts as a seemingly harmless act of avoidance can snowball into an insurmountable issue that could have been nipped in the bud. The pebble starts the avalanche, the spark that ignites the forest fire, and the drop overflows the cup.

Emotional Drain

Imagine carrying a backpack and adding a small rock whenever you avoid a conflict. It may feel manageable at first, but over time, those rocks become a heavy, draining burden that you lug around everywhere you go. The emotional toll of avoiding conflict is much the same. At first, it feels like you're maintaining peace, preserving your emotional energy. But you're stowing away chunks of emotional turmoil into your internal backpack. This emotional drain manifests in various ways: restlessness, perpetual dissatisfaction, irritability, and physical symptoms like headaches or sleeplessness. You're like a phone battery constantly running in low-power mode; you can perform the basic functions but can't operate at full capacity. The emotional drain saps your energy in your relationship and all aspects of life. It's like running a marathon with a sprained ankle; you might reach the finish line, but at what cost?

Consequences of Lack of Effective Conflict Resolution

Communication Breakdown

Communication is the lifeblood of any relationship, and a lack of effective conflict resolution acts like a clot, obstructing the free flow of understanding and mutual respect. When conflicts aren't resolved, it's akin to a linguistic Tower of Babel within the relationship; both parties speak, but neither understands. Conversations turn into exchanges of monologues, each person merely waiting for their turn to talk rather than actively listening. This breakdown is the starting point of many other issues, as it isolates partners within their emotional worlds, devoid of shared understanding.

Reduced Willingness to Communicate

Over time, the communication breakdown evolves into a reluctance even to engage. It's the emotional equivalent of pulling the covers over your head and hoping the problem disappears. The silence isn't just the absence of words; it's the absence of connection. This reduced willingness to communicate is like a fog that rolls in, making navigation perilous and obscuring the road ahead, ultimately leading the relationship down a path of stagnation and emotional estrangement.

Negative Emotional Consequences

The unresolved conflicts act like a Pandora's Box of negative emotions—resentment, anger, disappointment, and frustration. These emotions don't exist in a vacuum; they seep into every interaction, coloring even the happy moments with a shade of bitterness. Over time, this emotional cocktail can turn toxic, poisoning the relationship and affecting individual well-being.

Increased Defensiveness

When conflicts are left unresolved, the default mode becomes defensiveness. Each partner armors up, ready for battle, even when no conflict is apparent. This constant state of high alert is emotionally draining. It creates a perpetual cycle of offense and defense, a never-ending emotional tug-of-war that leaves both parties exhausted and unsatisfied.

Lack of Clarity

Without effective conflict resolution, the relationship becomes a maze with no clear exit. Simple questions like "What are we fighting about?" or "What do you want?" become impossible to answer. This lack of clarity turns every issue into a monster lurking in the shadows, far more terrifying than it needs to be.

Unwillingness to Compromise

When conflicts aren't resolved effectively, compromise becomes a dirty word. The relationship turns into a zero-sum game where one person's gain is viewed as another's loss. This unwillingness to compromise can make even the most straightforward issues insurmountable as both parties dig their heels in, prioritizing their egos over the relationship's well-being.

Loss of Trust

Trust, once broken, is incredibly hard to rebuild, and a lack of conflict resolution shatters trust like a hammer to glass. The absence of trust turns the relationship into a house of cards, unstable and ready to collapse at the slightest hint of wind.

Broken Promises

With unresolved conflicts come unkept promises. These broken promises act like termites, slowly eroding the foundations of trust and mutual respect until all left is a hollow shell of a relationship.

Lack of Transparency

When conflicts are avoided or poorly managed, transparency flies out the window. Secrets are kept, truths are bent, and a shroud of dishonesty descends upon the relationship. This lack of transparency can make each person feel like a detective in their relationship, constantly looking for clues instead of enjoying the journey together.

Perceived Betrayal

In a landscape rife with broken promises and lack of transparency, even small oversights or innocent mistakes can be perceived as betrayals. The narrative changes from "us against the problem" to "me against you," a destructive mindset that can spell the end for even the strongest relationships.

Emotional Manipulation

The ultimate cost of avoiding effective conflict resolution is the resort to emotional manipulation. Whether it's guilt-tripping, gaslighting, or passive-aggressive behavior, emotional manipulation is the death knell for genuine intimacy and mutual growth. It's the point of no return, where the relationship becomes a battleground, not of conflicting viewpoints, but of conflicting existences.

Impact Beyond the Relationship

Impact on Professional Life

When conflict remains unresolved in a relationship, it's like carrying a backpack full of stones into your workplace daily. The emotional turmoil doesn't clock out when you do; it follows you, influencing your interactions with colleagues, focus, and performance. You may be staring at a spreadsheet, but thinking about last night's argument. Or maybe you're in a meeting, but your mind is replaying the loop of what went wrong in your relationship. This mental preoccupation can lead to reduced productivity, distractions, and even increased stress, affecting not just you but also the dynamics of your professional environment.

Community and Social Impact

Unresolved conflicts in a relationship can also have a broader social impact. Friends and family often walk on eggshells around a couple constantly at odds. Social gatherings can become tense, uncomfortable affairs where everyone is hyper-aware of saying the "wrong thing" that might trigger a conflict. Over time, this tension can erode the sense of community, leading to isolation. In some cases, unresolved conflicts can even ripple out to affect community dynamics, such as involvement in social causes, religious activities, or community services.

Negative Impact on Mental Health

The emotional toll of unresolved conflict is not to be underestimated. The constant state of tension, the ceaseless "what ifs," and the never-ending cycle of blame and guilt can wreak havoc on mental health. Feelings of anxiety, depression, and even symptoms of post-traumatic stress disorder (PTSD) can manifest. The mental exhaustion from dealing with ongoing conflict can also lead to physical symptoms, such as headaches, digestive issues, and sleep disturbances. In a nutshell, the unresolved conflict doesn't just scar the relationship; it scars the individuals in it, affecting their overall well-being and quality of life.

Traditional Approaches to Conflict Resolution

Collaborative Approach

The collaborative approach is the golden child of conflict resolution strategies, often lauded as the ideal. Imagine a Venn diagram where one circle represents your interests and the other represents your partner's. The collaborative approach aims for that sweet spot in the middle—the intersection where both parties' needs and wants overlap. It's like cooking a meal together; each person contributes ingredients, and the final dish is something neither could have created alone. But be warned, this approach requires open communication, mutual respect, and a high degree of trust. It's not a sprint; it's a marathon, demanding sustained emotional stamina from both parties.

Compromising Approach

The compromising approach is the classic 'give a little, take a little' strategy. Picture it as a seesaw: balance is the goal, even if it means each person has to move a bit from their original position. It's the quick and often temporary fix, ideal for resolving conflicts where the stakes are not particularly high. The downside? Each party has to sacrifice something, and if not done judiciously, this can lead to long-term resentment or the feeling that one is constantly 'losing out' in the relationship.

Accommodating Approach

The accommodating approach could be likened to a surrender flag, where one party decides the issue is not worth a skirmish and accedes to the other's viewpoint. It's the 'Okay, let's do it your way' of conflict resolution. This approach can be a harmonious quick fix but comes with a major caveat: the accommodating party might accumulate feelings of being overlooked or unimportant, which can lead to emotional debt in the relationship.

Competing Approach

The competing approach is the gladiator arena of conflict resolution methods. One party wins; the other loses. It's a zero-sum game driven by power dynamics, often resorted to when one or both parties feel strongly about their stance and are unwilling to budge. While this approach may yield quick decisions, it often leaves a trail of emotional destruction. The 'loser' may harbor resentment, injustice, or disempowerment, casting a long shadow over the relationship.

Avoiding Approach

The avoiding approach is the ostrich strategy—stick your head in the sand and hope the problem disappears. On the surface, it might seem like the conflict has been diffused, but it's just been postponed. This approach is the emotional equivalent of sweeping dust under the rug; it might not be visible, but it's still there. Over time, these unresolved issues can pile up, leading to a major emotional reckoning.

Innovative Approaches to Conflict Resolution

Transformative Approach

The transformative approach to conflict resolution is like relationship alchemy. It aims to resolve the issue and fundamentally transform the relationship dynamics. It's an approach that believes every conflict presents an opportunity for individual and collective growth. Picture a garden; conflicts are the weeds. Instead of just plucking them out, the transformative approach digs deeper to enrich the soil, making it less likely for weeds to grow in the future. This method requires an almost metamorphic shift in perspective—from seeing conflicts as problems to be solved to viewing them as catalysts for change. It's about harnessing the energy of conflict to propel the relationship to new heights. This approach often incorporates emotional intelligence, empathy, and mutual respect. It's like upgrading your relationship software to be more adaptive, resilient, and harmonious.

Mindfulness-Based Techniques

Mindfulness-based techniques in conflict resolution are like taking a magnifying glass to the moment conflict arises. Instead of reacting impulsively, mindfulness teaches you to respond thoughtfully. Imagine your conflict is a turbulent sea; mindfulness is the anchor that keeps your emotional boat from being tossed around aimlessly. In practice, this could mean taking deep breaths to center yourself before responding to an accusation or perhaps engaging in 'mindful listening,' where you focus entirely on understanding your partner's perspective without mentally preparing your counter-argument. It's about being present, not just physically but emotionally and mentally. Creating this emotional space allows for more rational and compassionate discussions, free from the heat of momentary emotions. Mindfulness doesn't just defuse the conflict; it provides a toolkit for managing emotional reactions, offering a path toward resolution and personal growth. It turns conflict from a fire to be extinguished into a lamp, guiding the way to better understanding and deeper connection.

The Conflict Resolution Process

Identifying the Conflict

The first step in any conflict resolution process is akin to a diagnostic test in medicine—you need to identify the problem before you can treat it. This stage involves a heightened sense of awareness and emotional intelligence. It's about recognizing the subtle changes in interaction, the shifts in mood, or the unsaid words that hang in the air like an invisible fog. Ignoring or glossing over these signs is like slapping a band-aid on a wound that needs stitches; it might cover the problem temporarily but won't facilitate genuine healing.

Root Cause Analysis

Once the conflict has been identified, the next step is to dig deeper and unearth the root cause. Imagine you're an emotional archaeologist, sifting through layers of feelings, misunderstandings, and past experiences to get to the core issue. The apparent reason for the conflict is often just the tip of the iceberg. Beneath it lies a complex web of emotional needs, unmet expectations, or past unresolved issues. Conducting a thorough root cause analysis is like cleaning a wound before stitching it up; it's painful but necessary for long-term healing.

Notice Changes in Behavior

Monitoring behavioral changes is like being an emotional detective. It involves picking up on subtle cues that indicate a deeper issue. Maybe your partner is withdrawing or becoming more irritable. Perhaps conversations that used to be fluid and engaging now feel forced and stilted. These changes in behavior are the smoke signals of an underlying fire. They're the body's way of saying, 'Hey, something's not right here,' and paying attention to them can provide valuable insights into the nature and gravity of the conflict.

Identify Patterns

This stage is about connecting the dots. Conflicts rarely occur in isolation; they're usually part of a pattern of behavior or interaction. Identifying these patterns can provide a macro view of the relationship dynamics, revealing the 'what' and the 'why' behind recurring conflicts. It's like zooming out on a map to see the entire journey rather than just the bump in the road you're currently facing. Understanding these patterns can give both parties the tools to preempt future conflicts and engage in more constructive, empathetic interactions.

Emotional Triggers and Communication in Conflict Resolution

Emotional Triggers

Think of emotional triggers as invisible tripwires. They're seemingly innocuous words, actions, or situations that ignite an intense emotional reaction. It's like accidentally stepping on a landmine of emotions; one moment, everything is fine, and the next, it's chaos. These triggers often have deep roots in past experiences, insecurities, or unresolved issues. Identifying them is like mapping out a minefield; it helps to navigate the relationship terrain more safely.

Understanding and Navigating Emotional Triggers

The first step in dealing with emotional triggers is recognizing them. Imagine you're an emotional cartographer plotting out these sensitive spots on the map of your relationship. Knowing where they are is not just enough; you must also understand why they're there. Are they remnants from past relationships? Scars from childhood? Fears about the future? Understanding the 'why' gives you the roadmap to navigate around them. Navigating emotional triggers is like advanced driving lessons for the soul. It requires agility, awareness, and a lot of patience. Sometimes, it's about steering clear of known triggers; at other times, it's about diffusing a triggered situation through empathy and understanding. The key is to avoid and disarm the trigger, turning a potential explosion into an opportunity for deeper connection and understanding.

Communication in Conflict Resolution

Communication during conflict resolution is the bridge that connects two isolated islands of misunderstanding. It's the vehicle that carries both parties from a place of conflict to a haven of resolution. But remember, not all bridges are built the same, and not all vehicles suit the journey.

Choosing the Right Time and Place

When addressing conflict, timing and setting are not just details but game-changers. Imagine discussing a serious issue during a family gathering or before rushing to work. The chaos or stress of the environment can seep into the conversation, escalating the conflict rather than resolving it. Choosing the right time and place is like setting the stage for a heartfelt drama; the setting can either enhance or detract from the performance. It should be a time and place where both parties can be fully present physically, emotionally, and mentally. It's like finding a quiet harbor amidst a storm, a space where the winds of external distractions can't touch the sails of your deep conversation.

Use of 'I' Statements

The language we use in conflict can be a balm or a spark. Using 'I' statements is akin to choosing silk over sandpaper; it's softer, kinder, and far less likely to irritate. When you frame your feelings and perspectives with 'I feel,' 'I think,' or 'I believe,' you own your emotions rather than projecting them onto your partner. It's like handing someone an open book instead of a loaded gun. It invites understanding rather than defensiveness, opening the door for a conversation rather than an argument.

The Power of Personal Ownership

'I' statements are more than just a linguistic choice; they declare personal ownership and responsibility. When you say, 'I feel hurt when you do that,' instead of 'You hurt me,' you're shifting the focus from blaming to explaining. It's like comparing a spotlight to a floodlight; one pinpoint while the other illuminates. By illuminating your feelings and reactions, you give the other person a chance to understand your perspective without feeling attacked.

Active Listening

Active listening is the verbal equivalent of holding someone's hand; it's a reassuring, guiding presence that makes all the difference. In a conflict-filled conversation, becoming preoccupied with your next counter-argument is easy. Active listening encourages you to park that impulse and fully immerse yourself in understanding the other person's viewpoint. It's like choosing to walk in their shoes to understand their journey better, even if just for a moment.

The Art of Presence

Active listening is more than just hearing; it's about being emotionally and mentally present. It's about catching every word, understanding the tone, and reading between the lines. It involves acknowledging, either verbally or through body language, that you are fully engaged in the conversation. This level of attention is like a gift in a world of distractions and can significantly enhance the quality of any dialogue.

Avoiding Interruptions

Cutting someone off mid-sentence is the conversational equivalent of slamming a door in their face. It's abrupt, startling, and instantly puts the other person on the defensive. Avoiding interruptions is not just good manners; it's an act of respect. It sends a clear message that you value what the other person says and are willing to wait your turn to speak.

The Virtue of Patience

Avoiding interruptions requires patience, a virtue that's often in short supply during heated discussions. This restraint is like holding back a floodgate of words and emotions to allow space for something more meaningful to flow. It enables a fuller, richer dialogue where both parties can express themselves without the fear of being silenced.

Assertiveness, Identifying Common Ground, and Role of Emotional Intelligence

Assertiveness and Its Role

Assertiveness is the golden mean between passivity and aggression—a balanced approach that empowers you to express your needs and opinions clearly without disregarding those of others. Think of it as being the conductor of your emotional orchestra. You're in control, but you're also tuned in to the needs and contributions of others, harmonizing the relationship rather than creating discord.

The Fine Line Between Confidence and Respect

Assertiveness strikes a delicate balance between confidence and respect. It's like standing your ground while acknowledging the boundaries of others. Being assertive doesn't mean steamrolling over others to get your way. It means having the courage to express your needs and opinions while also having the empathy to listen to and respect the needs of others. It's the conversational version of ballroom dancing—leading when necessary but always in step with your partner.

Identifying Common Ground

Finding common ground is like discovering an oasis in the desert of conflict. It's that refreshing spot where both parties can unite for relief and sustenance. Identifying areas of agreement or shared values can provide a solid foundation to build a resolution.

The Power of Unity in Division

Even when disagreements seem impossible, there's usually some aspect—no matter how small—where both parties can find agreement. Focusing on these shared points can change the dynamic of the conversation. It's like finding a patch of solid ground amidst a dilemma; it may not solve all your problems, but it provides a stable point to navigate the more challenging issues.

Role of Emotional Intelligence

Emotional intelligence is the unsung hero of conflict resolution. It's your internal diplomat, mediating between your needs and those of others. Emotional intelligence allows you to read, understand, and respond to emotional cues—both yours and those of the people around you.

A Symphony of Understanding

Think of emotional intelligence as the conductor of a symphony of interpersonal interactions. It helps you tune into the emotional undertones, pick up on unspoken cues, and respond sensitively and effectively. It's like having a sixth sense of the emotional landscape of a situation, enabling you to navigate it with greater ease and effectiveness.

Solution-Based Techniques in Conflict Resolution

Solution-Based Techniques

When conflicts arise, it's easy to get ensnared in a thorny thicket of blame, emotions, and endless 'what-ifs.' Solution-based techniques offer a way out. Picture them as the machete that clears a path through the dense jungle of discord, leading the way to the open meadow of resolution and understanding.

In conflict, it's natural to zoom in on the problem, dissecting its every facet. Solution-based techniques encourage us to turn the telescope around and look at the bigger picture. Instead of fixing what went wrong, the focus shifts to what can be done to make it right.

Brainstorming Solutions

Brainstorming is the creative furnace where raw ideas are melted down and recast into innovative solutions. Imagine this stage as an alchemist's lab, where ordinary thoughts transform into golden opportunities.

Brainstorming is not merely a hailstorm of thoughts; it's an alchemical process. Regardless of its initial luster, each idea contributes to the end product. It's a judgment-free zone where the most eccentric thoughts often become the catalysts for groundbreaking solutions.

Setting Ground Rules

If brainstorming is the furnace, then ground rules are the safety protocols. They ensure that the creative heat doesn't turn into a destructive blaze. Consider them the foundational pillars that uphold the integrity of the conflict resolution process.

Ground rules serve as the architectural blueprint for constructive dialogue. They outline the boundaries within which the conversation should occur, safeguarding the structural integrity of the conflict resolution process. Whether it's a rule against shouting or a mutual agreement to avoid blame, these ground rules are the non-negotiables that keep the dialogue civil and productive.

Generating and Evaluating Ideas

This stage is the crucible where brainstormed ideas endure the tests of feasibility, impact, and practicality. It's like a reality TV elimination round, where only the strongest contenders survive. The process of generating and evaluating ideas is Darwinian. Ideas compete for survival, subjected to rigorous tests of validity and utility. It's not enough for an idea to be innovative; it must also be implementable, beneficial, and acceptable to all parties involved.

Implementing the Solution

Here's where the proverbial rubber meets the road. All the brainstorming, ground rules, and evaluations culminate in a plan ready for action. Think of this stage as the grand finale, the final act where ideas take the stage in the real world. In the implementation phase, your meticulously designed blueprint turns into a tangible structure. Agreeing on a solution is one thing, but executing it requires a coordinated effort, clear roles, and actionable steps. It's the culmination of theory into practice, a transformative process that converts the abstract into the concrete.

Final Stages in Conflict Resolution

Communicating the Solution

Finding a solution is like discovering a treasure; it's valuable but useless if kept hidden. Communication is the vehicle that carries this treasure from the confines of a meeting room to the landscape of real-life application. Think of this stage as translating a complex formula into everyday language. It's not just about saying, 'We've found a solution,' but explaining what it is, how it works, and what it means for everyone involved. It's like turning the complex notes of a symphony into a tune that everyone can hum.

Getting Buy-In

Buy-in is the electric charge that powers the machinery of any solution. The collective yes, the chorus of agreement that turns a plan from ink on paper to a living, breathing course of action. Getting buy-in is more than nodding heads; it's about emotional and intellectual investment. It's like turning shareholders into stakeholders. When people are bought in, they're not just agreeing to a plan—they're adopting it as their own, rooting for its success as they would for a personal endeavor.

Establishing a Timeline

A timeline is the skeleton that supports the flesh and blood of your solution. It turns a wish into a goal, a possibility into a plan. Think of the timeline as the gears in a clock. Each cog, no matter how small, plays a role in keeping time. Specific deadlines and milestones serve as checkpoints, helping everyone stay in sync and ensuring the solution rolls out as smoothly as clockwork.

Assigning Responsibilities

This is where the abstract becomes concrete. Assigning responsibilities is like casting roles in a play. Everyone knows their lines, cues, and responsibilities, ensuring the performance succeeds. Assigning responsibilities is the choreography that ensures the dance of implementation is graceful, coordinated, and effective. Each person knows their steps and how those steps contribute to the overall performance.

Future-Proofing Solutions

This is your safety net, the seat belt that keeps you secure as you navigate the winding roads of interpersonal relationships. Future-proofing is like designing a building to withstand the current climate and future environmental changes. It's about incorporating flexibility and adaptability, ensuring the solution is not a one-hit-wonder but a long-lasting hit.

Feedback Loop

The feedback loop is the built-in mechanism for continual improvement. It turns a solution into a living entity capable of evolving and adapting. Imagine the feedback loop as a spiral staircase. Each loop is an opportunity to ascend to a higher level of understanding and efficiency. It's not about going in circles but rising upward, turning each challenge into a stepping stone for future growth.

Enhancing Communication Skills

Imagine communication skills as the Swiss Army knife in your social toolbox—versatile, indispensable, and always reliable. These skills are not just the basic 'hello' and 'goodbye,' but the intricate art of conveying complex thoughts, emotions, and intentions in a way that's as clear as a mountain stream.

Enhancing communication skills is like fine-tuning a musical instrument. Each note, each chord, must resonate in harmony with the other. And just like a musician studies scales and compositions, mastering the art of communication involves a deep understanding of its various components, from verbal cues to non-verbal gestures.

Learning Effective Communication Skills

Effective communication is not an inherited trait but a learned skill. It's like learning to cook; you start with the basics and then add your flavors as you get more comfortable. Think of learning communication skills as following a recipe. Each ingredient represents a different skill, and combining them in the right proportions can create a masterpiece of meaningful interaction.

Active Listening

Active listening is the unsung hero of communication. It's not merely about hearing words but understanding the emotions, intentions, and subtext behind them. Imagine active listening as holding up a mirror to the speaker's thoughts, reflecting what is said and meant. It's about reading between the lines, catching the undertones, and understanding the unspoken.

Empathy

Empathy is walking in someone else's shoes without getting your feet dirty. It's about feeling, seeing what they see, and understanding their point of view. Think of empathy as building an invisible bridge between hearts and minds. It's not about losing yourself in another's emotions but about extending a hand of understanding across the chasm that often separates human experience.

Clarity

In the complex dance of human interaction, clarity is your choreographer. It sets the steps, cues the moves, and ensures that both parties dance to the same tune. Imagine clarity as a lens that focuses the diffuse light of thoughts and feelings into a concentrated beam of understanding. Whether you're expressing love, disappointment, or anything in between, clarity ensures that your message hits its mark, bright and clear.

Understanding Nonverbal Communication

Nonverbal communication is the secret sauce that flavors every interaction, the electricity that powers the complex machinery of human relationships. It's the paint that colors the canvas of our words, adding depth, texture, and nuance. Think of nonverbal cues as the invisible ink on a letter. They might not be readily apparent, but under the right light—voila!—the true message appears. And just like invisible ink requires a special light to be seen, nonverbal cues often require special attention to be understood.

Body Language

Ah, the grand theatre of limbs and facial expressions! Body language is the Shakespearean drama of nonverbal communication, full of monologues, plot twists, and dramatic reveals. Imagine body language as a choreographed dance where every move has a meaning. A crossed arm might be a defensive shield, while an open palm can signal honesty. It's like interpretive dance but with everyday interactions instead of a stage.

Tone of Voice

It's not what you say but how you say it. Your voice is the background music to your words, setting the mood and tempo. Your tone is the melody that can make even a grocery list sound like a love song or a simple 'hello' feel like a hug. The inflection turns a question into an accusation, a sentence into a caress. If words are the lyrics, the tone is the tune.

Proximity

This is the invisible bubble of personal space we all carry around, and heaven help those who burst it uninvited! Think of proximity as the geography of a conversation. Too close, and you're invading; too far, and you're distancing yourself. It's about finding that sweet spot where intimacy and independence coexist.

Touch

A touch can be worth a thousand words. It can comfort, reassure, or ignite passion. But wielded poorly, it can also invade, intimidate, or offend. Consider each type of touch as a letter in a tactile alphabet. A hug is an 'A,' a pat on the back is a 'B,' and so on. Combine them correctly, and you can write sentences without saying a word. But be careful with your syntax; misplaced touches can turn poetry into gibberish.

Appearance

Last but not least, let's talk about the book cover to your story—your appearance. It's the first chapter people read, setting the stage for everything that follows. Your appearance is your visual resume, providing a snapshot of who you are—or at least who you want to appear to be. The wardrobe choices can make you look 'business casual' or 'weekend ready,' and the grooming touches that say 'I care' or 'I couldn't be bothered.'

Your Personalized Workbook

While this workbook offers a structured approach, it's designed to be flexible. The exercises provided don't have to be taken in the order they are listed. Feel free to pick and choose exercises that resonate with you and are most appropriate for the specific challenges or circumstances you're facing. Consider this workbook as a menu of options, not a set sequence of steps.

Chapter Exercises

Exercise: Conflict Archetypes

Introduction

It's often said that history repeats itself, and if you've been in a relationship long enough, you've probably noticed that conflicts do, too. Whether it's another heated 'discussion' about finances or the umpteenth argument about household chores, recurring conflicts can be like that annoying song on repeat—you're over it, but it just keeps playing. The Conflict Archetypes exercise helps you identify these 'hit singles' of discord in your relationship and find ways to change the tune or learn to dance to it.

Objective

To identify recurring conflicts in the relationship and discuss the underlying issues. By understanding the archetypes of your conflicts, you can work towards more effective resolutions and a harmonious relationship.

Materials Needed
- A quiet, comfortable space for discussion
- Pen and paper for jotting down thoughts
- An open mind (essential!)

Time Required

45-60 minutes. Consider it an investment in relationship harmony.

Instructions
1. **Discussion and Identification:** Sit down with your partner and start discussing your conflicts. Try to identify recurring themes or types of conflicts. Use the archetypes listed below as a guide.
2. **Categorize into Archetypes:** Once you've discussed past conflicts, try to categorize them into archetypes. Use the list of Conflict Archetypes to help you.
3. **Root Cause Analysis:** Discuss the root causes for each conflict archetype. Why do these specific conflicts keep happening? Is there a deeper issue that needs to be addressed?

4. **Brainstorm Solutions:** After identifying the root causes, brainstorm possible solutions for each type of conflict. These could be immediate actions or long-term plans.

Conflict Archetypes
1. Financial Conflicts
These conflicts often revolve around how money is spent, saved, or invested. They can manifest as disagreements over big expenditures, budgeting, or financial priorities.

2. Emotional Needs
These conflicts arise when unmet emotional needs like affection, validation, or attention are unmet.

3. Household Responsibilities
These conflicts often occur when there's an imbalance in the division of household chores, childcare, or other responsibilities.

4. Communication Style
Conflicts over communication style happen when there's a mismatch in how both partners express themselves or handle disagreements.

Reflection and Takeaways
After completing this exercise, take a moment to reflect. Did categorizing your conflicts into archetypes offer any revelations? Were you able to pinpoint root causes and come up with viable solutions? Use these insights as a roadmap for navigating future conflicts. After all, if you know the terrain, you're less likely to get lost.

Exercise: The Fair Fight Rules

Introduction
Ah, the art of argument! While disagreements are a natural part of any relationship, how you argue makes all the difference. Throwing dishes may be dramatic, but it's hardly constructive. The Fair Fight Rules exercise aims to level the playing field, ensuring that conflicts are resolved in a healthy, constructive manner. Consider this the rulebook for your relationship's 'emotional sportsmanship.'

Objective

Establish a set of 'fair fight' rules that both partners agree to follow during conflicts. These rules serve as guidelines for respectful and effective communication during disagreements.

Materials Needed

- A quiet, comfortable space for discussion
- Pen and paper for jotting down your agreed-upon rules
- A commitment to play fair (No low blows!)

Time Required

30-45 minutes. Remember, fair play leads to a winning relationship.

Instructions

1. **Discuss Common Pitfalls:** Discuss common pitfalls during your arguments. This could be anything from raising voices to bringing up unrelated past issues.
2. **Create Fair Fight Rules:** Based on your discussion, create a list of rules you agree to adhere to during conflicts. This could include points like 'no yelling' or 'staying on topic.'
3. **Role-Play:** Role-play a conflict scenario once your rules are established. Make sure to abide by the Fair Fight Rules. After the role-play, discuss how following the rules impacted the argument.

Reflection and Takeaways

After establishing your Fair Fight Rules and practicing them through role-play, reflect on the experience. Did having set guidelines to make the conflict easier to navigate? Were both partners able to adhere to the rules? Keep these rules handy—literally or figuratively—as you tackle future disagreements. They're your relationship's playbook, ensuring that every conflict has the potential for a win-win outcome.

Exercise 3: The Conflict De-escalation Plan

Introduction

Ever feel like your arguments escalate faster than a rocket launch? One minute, you're talking about who forgot to take out the trash; the next, you're questioning the entire relationship. Conflicts are inevitable, but escalation isn't. The Conflict De-escalation Plan is designed to help you put on the brakes before reaching emotional orbit.

Objective

This exercise aims to create a step-by-step plan for de-escalating conflicts. Identifying triggers and establishing calming strategies can keep disagreements from spiraling out of control.

Materials Needed

- A quiet, comfortable space for discussion
- Pen and paper or an electronic device for note-taking
- A willingness to keep things cool (literally and metaphorically)

Time Required

30-45 minutes. It's a small time investment for a big emotional payoff.

Instructions

1. **Discuss Triggers:** Begin by discussing the triggers that commonly escalate conflicts between you. This can include things like raising voices, name-calling, or going off-topic.
2. **Develop a De-escalation Plan:** Once you've identified the triggers, work together to create a de-escalation plan. This should include specific actions or phrases when a trigger is activated.
3. **Role-Play:** Role-play a conflict scenario using the de-escalation plan after developing the plan. Discuss how effective the strategies were and adjust as needed.

Reflection and Takeaways

Following the role-play, take a moment to reflect. How effective was the de-escalation plan in keeping the conflict from spiraling? Are there areas for improvement? Keep this plan accessible and use it as a reference during future conflicts. In time, these strategies will become second nature, making every disagreement an opportunity for growth rather than a battle.

Exercise 5: Post-Conflict Reflections

Introduction

Let's face it: conflicts aren't fun. But, like a challenging workout, they can be extremely beneficial if you take the time to reflect and learn from them. Post-conflict reflections are the relationship equivalent of a post-game analysis. It's where you look at the 'game tape' of your disagreements and figure out what plays worked, what didn't, and how you can improve for next time.

Objective
This exercise aims to reflect on resolved conflicts for learning and growth. You can gain valuable insights into navigating future disagreements better by analyzing what worked and what didn't.

Materials Needed
- A quiet, comfortable space for reflection and discussion
- Pen and paper or an electronic device for notetaking
- A commitment to personal and relational growth

Time Required
20-30 minutes. Because hindsight is 20/20, and this is time well spent.

Instructions
1. **Choose a Conflict:** Select a recently resolved conflict for analysis. Make sure it's something both parties are comfortable discussing.
2. **Discuss What Worked:** Talk about the aspects of the conflict resolution that were effective. Was it open communication? Empathy? What led to a resolution?
3. **Discuss What Didn't Work:** Equally important is to talk about what didn't work. Were there moments of escalation? Did someone resort to blame or name-calling?
4. **Identify Lessons Learned:** After discussing the pros and cons, identify the lessons learned and areas where you can improve in future conflicts.

Reflection and Takeaways
Once you've gone through your post-conflict reflections, you're better equipped to handle future disagreements. Like any practice, the better you get, the more you do it. So the next time a conflict arises, remember: it's not just a disagreement; it's an opportunity for growth.

Exercise 6: The Empathy Exercise

Introduction
Empathy is the emotional superglue of any relationship. It's the ability to understand and share your partner's feelings, creating a sense of connection and closeness. The Empathy Exercise aims to go beyond the 'I'm sorry you feel that way' and into the realm of 'I understand how you feel, and here's why it matters to me.'

Objective

This exercise aims to practice empathy by understanding the emotional needs of each partner during conflict. By diving deep into the emotional currents of your disagreements, you'll better understand each other and find more compassionate ways to resolve conflicts.

Materials Needed

- A quiet, comfortable space for open dialogue
- Pen and paper or an electronic device for notetaking
- An empathetic ear and an open heart

Time Required

30-45 minutes. Because understanding is the first step to acceptance, which is the key to harmony.

Instructions

1. **Share a Conflict:** Share a recent conflict where emotions ran high. Describe the situation and how each of you felt during the disagreement.
2. **Discuss Emotions and Needs:** Take turns discussing the emotions and needs at play for each person. Try to do this without interruption or judgment.
3. **Explore Empathy:** Discuss how empathy during the conflict could have led to a different outcome. Could understanding each other's emotional needs have defused the situation?

Reflection and Takeaways

Reflect on how empathy—or the lack thereof—played a role in the conflict. Did this exercise bring to light any emotional needs you weren't aware of? Remember, empathy is a skill that can be developed and refined. Use what you've learned here to bring more empathy into future interactions during conflicts and peaceful times.

Exercise 7: The Timeout Technique

Introduction

Sometimes, not having one is the best way to win a fight. Easier said than done, right? Well, that's where the Timeout Technique comes in. Think of it as the adult version of being sent to your room to 'think about what you've done,' but with mutual consent and without the lingering resentment. It's a way to hit the pause button on escalating conflicts, allowing both parties to cool off and return to the issue with clearer heads.

Objective

This exercise aims to establish a 'timeout' method for pausing and reflecting during heated conflicts. By agreeing on a specific signal and set of rules for timeouts, you can prevent conflicts from escalating into full-blown emotional meltdowns.

Materials Needed
- A quiet, comfortable space for discussion
- Pen and paper or an electronic device for notetaking
- A timer (optional but useful for timed timeouts)

Time Required

20-30 minutes. Timeouts aren't just for kids or sports but also for relationships.

Instructions
1. **Discuss Signals:** Discuss the signals that indicate a conflict is becoming too heated. These could be physical cues, verbal expressions, or specific behaviors.
2. **Agree on a Timeout Signal:** Choose a signal that either partner can use to initiate a timeout. This could be a word, a hand gesture, or even a humorous prop.
3. **Establish Timeout Rules:** Agree on the rules for taking a timeout. How long will it last? Is there a designated space to retreat to? What are the expectations for re-engaging?
4. **Role-Play:** Role-play a conflict scenario and practice using the timeout method. Reflect on how it felt to pause and whether it helped to defuse the situation.

Reflection and Takeaways

After the role-play, reflect on the effectiveness of the Timeout Technique. Did it help to prevent escalation? Were both partners able to respect the timeout? This tool is as useful as you make it, so commit to using it responsibly and respectfully.

Exercise 8: Conflict Journaling

Introduction

Just as athletes track their workouts and nutritionists log food intake, tracking your conflicts can offer valuable insights into your relationship. Conflict Journaling isn't about keeping score but identifying patterns and triggers. Consider it your personal 'black box' recorder, capturing the details that lead to turbulence so you can navigate smoother skies ahead.

Objective

This exercise aims to keep a journal of conflicts to better understand patterns, triggers, and emotional states over time. You can develop strategies for more effective conflict resolution by monitoring these elements.

Materials Needed

- A dedicated journal or electronic document for tracking conflicts
- A pen or electronic device for journal entries
- A commitment to honest, non-judgmental reflection

Time Required

Ongoing. Consistency is key for meaningful insights.

Instructions

1. **Introduce the Idea:** Discuss the idea of Conflict Journaling and agree on the commitment to track conflicts for a specified period.
2. **Choose Metrics:** Decide what metrics to track. This could include the cause of the conflict, emotional state, escalation triggers, and resolution strategies.
3. **Keep Journaling:** Each time a conflict arises, make a journal entry detailing the agreed-upon metrics. Be as specific and honest as possible.
4. **Review:** Periodically review the journal entries to identify patterns, triggers, and opportunities for improvement.

Reflection and Takeaways

After a set period of journaling, take the time to review your entries together. Are there recurring issues that need to be addressed? Have certain conflict resolution strategies proven more effective than others? Use these insights to refine your conflict approach and improve your relationship overall.

Exercise 9: The Apology Workshop

Introduction

Saying 'I'm sorry' is easy; giving a meaningful apology is an art. In the Apology Workshop, you'll explore the elements of an effective apology. This isn't just about uttering the words 'I'm sorry.' It's about understanding the impact of your actions, taking responsibility, and committing to change. Because a well-crafted apology doesn't just mend fences; it builds stronger ones.

Objective

This exercise aims to explore the elements of a sincere and effective apology. By understanding and practicing the components of a genuine apology, you'll be better equipped to mend rifts and strengthen your relationship.

Materials Needed

- A quiet, comfortable space for discussion
- Pen and paper or an electronic device for notetaking
- A willingness to be vulnerable and honest

Time Required

30-45 minutes. A small investment for big relationship dividends.

Instructions

1. **Discuss Components:** Start by discussing the components of a meaningful apology. This can include acknowledging the hurt caused, taking responsibility, and outlining steps to prevent recurrence.
2. **Role-Play Scenarios:** Choose scenarios that require an apology and role-play them. One partner can act as the 'offender' and the other as the 'receiver' of the apology.
3. **Evaluate:** After each role-play, discuss the effectiveness of the apology. Was it sincere? Did it address the key components of a meaningful apology? Adjust as needed.

Reflection and Takeaways
Reflect on the exercise and discuss any revelations or improvements. Did the role-play scenarios make you more aware of the intricacies involved in apologizing? Remember, a meaningful apology is one of the most powerful tools in maintaining a healthy relationship. Make it count.

Exercise 10: The "What's Left Unsaid" Exploration

Introduction
The loudest words in a relationship are often the ones that go unspoken. These unvoiced thoughts, feelings, and concerns can be ticking time bombs, waiting for the right (or wrong) moment to explode. The 'What's Left Unsaid' Exploration is your bomb-defusing kit. This exercise aims to create a safe space where you and your partner can bring those unspoken issues into the open. It's like giving voice to the silent characters in your relationship's narrative, adding depth and complexity to your mutual understanding.

Objective
This exercise aims to identify and openly discuss issues or feelings that haven't yet been voiced. Doing so will pre-empt potential conflicts and strengthen the emotional connection between you and your partner.

Materials Needed
- A quiet, comfortable space for discussion
- Writing materials (pen and paper or electronic devices)
- It's a 'judgment-free zone' sign, even if it's just a mental one.

Time Required
45-60 minutes. Like a good novel, the depth of exploration is worth the time invested.

Instructions
1. **Set the Scene:** Find a comfortable, quiet space where you and your partner can focus on each other. Establish that this is a 'judgment-free zone.' In this space, honesty is the best policy, but empathy is the golden rule.

2. **Individual Reflection:** Take 10-15 minutes for individual reflection. Each of you should write down any issues, concerns, or feelings that you haven't yet shared with your partner. These could range from minor annoyances to bigger, more complex issues.

3. **Share and Discuss:** Take turns sharing what you wrote down. The partner who is listening should do so actively, without interrupting. Keep the 'judgment-free zone' rule in mind throughout this process.

4. **Constructive Conversation:** After both partners have shared, move into a constructive conversation. Discuss each point, explore why it was left unsaid, and determine how to address it moving forward.

5. **Action Plan:** Based on your discussion, create a simple action plan. What steps can you both take to address the issues that were brought up? Remember, the plan doesn't have to be a grand manifesto; small, achievable steps are often more effective.

Reflection and Takeaways

After you've both shared and discussed the 'unsaid,' reflect on the experience. Did it feel liberating to get those hidden thoughts and feelings out in the open? Did you learn something new about your partner or gain a deeper understanding of their concerns? Commit to keeping this newfound openness alive in your relationship. Because when nothing is left unsaid, the story of your relationship becomes a richer, more engaging read.

Exercise 11: The "Active Listening" Challenge

Introduction

Have you ever had a conversation where you felt like you were talking to a brick wall? If so, you're not alone. Listening is an art form that many of us could stand to improve. In the heat of conflict, especially, it's easy to forget how to listen—really listen—to your partner. That's where the 'Active Listening' Challenge comes in. This exercise will fine-tune your listening skills and make you more attuned to your partner's needs and feelings. And who knows? You might discover that listening is more enlightening than speaking.

Objective

This exercise aims to practice the essential skill of active listening. By dedicating yourself to truly understanding what your partner is saying, you're laying the groundwork for more effective and empathetic communication. And let's be honest, who doesn't want that in a relationship?

Materials Needed

- A quiet, comfortable space for discussion
- A topic to discuss (ideally, something neutral to keep the focus on listening)
- A timer (your phone will do)

Time Required

20-30 minutes. It's a small investment of time for a potentially game-changing skill.

Instructions

1. **Choose a Topic:** Begin by selecting a topic to discuss. It could be anything from your plans for the weekend to a recent movie you watched. The idea is to keep it neutral so you can focus solely on the listening aspect.
2. **Set the Timer:** Set a timer for 5-10 minutes for each person. During this time, one person will speak while the other listens—actively.
3. **Listen Actively:** While your partner speaks, your role is to listen. And we mean listen. No interrupting, no preparing your response, and no scrolling through your phone. Nod, make eye contact, and give verbal cues like 'I understand' or 'Tell me more.'
4. **Summarize and Ask:** Once the timer goes off, summarize what you've heard and ask any clarifying questions. The speaker should then confirm whether the summary is accurate or offer corrections.
5. **Switch Roles:** After the first round, repeat the process. The listener now becomes the speaker, and vice versa.

Reflection and Takeaways

Once the exercise is complete, take a moment to discuss the experience. Was it challenging to listen without interrupting or formulating your responses? Did you find active listening gave you a deeper understanding of your partner's perspective? Reflect on these questions and think about how you can incorporate active listening into your daily interactions. After all, a good listener hears the words and catches what's left unsaid.

Exercise 12: The Conflict Resolution Role Reversal

Introduction

Have you ever wondered what walking a mile in your partner's shoes is like, especially during a heated argument? Please wear your metaphorical (and perhaps emotional) hiking boots because we're about to find out. The Conflict Resolution, Role Reversal exercise is a chance to gain a fresh perspective on conflicts by switching roles with your partner. Think of it as a role-playing game; instead of slaying dragons, you're conquering misunderstandings and breaking down emotional barriers.

Objective

This exercise aims to understand conflicts from your partner's perspective. By stepping into their shoes, you'll gain insights into their thoughts, feelings, and perhaps even the logic (or lack thereof) behind their actions during conflicts.

Materials Needed
  • A quiet, comfortable space for discussion
  • Open minds and hearts (yes, they're crucial materials!)

Time Required

30-45 minutes. Time flies when you're having fun...or gaining invaluable relationship insights!

Instructions
1. **Pick a Past Conflict:** Start by recalling a past conflict that both of you remember well. It could be anything from a trivial disagreement about what movie to watch to a more serious debate about life goals. Just make sure it's a conflict that has been resolved, so you're not reopening old wounds.
2. **Role Reversal:** Switch roles with your partner. You'll argue from their point of view, and they'll argue from yours. This may feel a bit like a theater rehearsal, but it's one where understanding, not entertainment, is the end goal.
3. **The Argument:** Reenact the argument from your chosen roles. Stick to the script, but also try to bring in the emotions and reasoning you believe your partner had during the original conflict. No overacting, please. This isn't a soap opera!

4. **Debrief:** Discuss what you each felt and learned after the role-reversal argument. Was it strange to argue against your point? Did you discover any 'aha' moments or gain surprising insights into your partner's perspective?

Reflection and Takeaways

So, how was the role-reversal experience? Was it like looking into a mirror and seeing a different reflection, or was it more of an 'alternate universe' experience? Either way, discuss the insights you both gained and how you can use this newfound understanding in future conflicts. Remember, the key to a successful relationship isn't avoiding conflicts; navigating through them effectively. And sometimes, all it takes to find the right path is a change in perspective.

Exercise 13: The Conflict Timeline

Introduction

Relationship conflicts are like plot twists in a riveting novel—unexpected, challenging, and sometimes downright frustrating. But what if you had a roadmap to help you navigate these tricky twists and turns? Introducing the Conflict Timeline—a visual tool designed to give you and your partner a bird's-eye view of your relationship's conflict landscape. Think of it as your personal 'conflict weather forecast,' enabling you to spot the storm clouds before they break into a full-blown cyclone.

Objective

In this eye-opening exercise, you and your partner will create a timeline to visualize the events leading to conflicts. By doing so, you'll identify patterns, triggers, and all the little gremlins that magically appear whenever a disagreement breeds. This is your chance to play detective in your own love story, hunting for clues that can help you pre-empt conflicts or, at the very least, navigate them more gracefully.

Materials Needed
- A large sheet of paper or a whiteboard
- Different colored markers or pens
- Sticky notes
- A calendar for reference

Time Required
60-90 minutes. Trust us; it's an hour (or so) well spent.

Instructions
1. **Setting the Stage:** Sit down with your partner in a quiet space where you can spread out your timeline. Make sure each of you has a marker or pen of a different color. Trust me, this isn't an art project, but the colors will help differentiate your inputs.
2. **Draw the Timeline:** Draw a long horizontal line on your paper or whiteboard. This line represents the last month of your relationship. Mark the start and end dates at the respective ends.
3. **Marking Conflicts:** With your partner, take turns recalling and marking points on the timeline where conflicts occurred. Use your colored markers to denote who was the 'initiator' of each conflict. Was it a dispute over household chores? Or maybe a disagreement about weekend plans? Whatever it was, mark it down.
4. **Annotate Each Point:** Use sticky notes to jot down additional details for each marked conflict point. Note the triggers, the emotions involved, and the eventual outcome. Was there shouting? Tears? A dramatic exit? Or perhaps a silent treatment session that would give a mime artist a run for their money?
5. **Pattern Recognition:** Once all conflict points are marked and annotated, step back and look for patterns. Are conflicts more frequent on weekends? Do they often stem from financial worries? Or perhaps they always occur when one of you is stressed or tired?
6. **Discussion:** After identifying patterns, discuss them openly with your partner. What can you both do to avoid or handle these triggers better in the future? This is your 'ah-ha!' moment, where you both realize that conflicts aren't random; they have their twisted logic. And that's something you can work with.

Reflection and Takeaways
After completing this exercise, take a moment to reflect on the experience. Was it eye-opening to see your conflicts laid out like episodes in a dramatic TV series? More importantly, did you identify any recurring villains—those annoying triggers—that seem to make a guest appearance in every conflict episode?

Please discuss with your partner what you can do differently to avoid or manage these conflicts more effectively. Keep your annotated timeline somewhere visible as a constant reminder that conflicts, much like bad weather, can be forecasted and prepared for.

Maintaining A Secure and Emotionally Connected Relationship

Brief Overview

Ah, validation! That magical elixir can turn a mundane conversation into an emotional banquet and a troubled relationship into a sanctuary of trust. No, it's not the latest trend in artisanal coffee or a mythical potion from ancient love stories. It's an everyday practice, grounded in psychological research, that has the power to make or break relationships.

Validation is the art and science of making someone feel heard, seen, and valid. In simpler terms, it's like saying, 'I see you, I hear you, and you make sense'—even if you don't agree with what the other person is saying or feeling. Think of it as the emotional equivalent of looking someone directly in the eye during a handshake: firm, sincere, and impossible to ignore.

So, why is this concept important in relationships? Well, human beings are social creatures. Our brains are hardwired to seek connection, and there's no quicker way to create disconnection than to make someone feel invalidated. Imagine you're sharing a concern with your partner, and they respond casually, 'Oh, you're overthinking it.' Ouch! It's like emotional whiplash. Suddenly, not only is the original problem still there, but now there's a new one: you're ostensibly in a relationship with a robot who doesn't understand feelings.

Validation is a relational glue that binds emotional experiences, creating a secure base for both partners. It allows couples to traverse the rocky terrains of misunderstandings, disappointments, and, dare we say, the occasional bad mood without falling into the abyss of eternal relationship doom. It's the scaffolding upon which you can construct an enduring and enriching relationship.

In this chapter, we'll dissect the what, why, and how of validation. We'll explore its psychological underpinnings, practical applications, and the common pitfalls that make you go from a validating superhero to an emotional villain. And, because we're in the business of 'keeping it real,' we'll sprinkle in some interactive exercises that are as entertaining as they are enlightening.

Objective of the Chapter

To put it mildly, navigating the labyrinthine corridors of a relationship without a flashlight or a map can be a Herculean task. It's akin to assembling an IKEA bookshelf without the instruction manual: you might eventually figure it out, but not without a few screw-ups (and perhaps a minor existential crisis) along the way.

That's where this chapter comes in. Consider it your instruction manual, map, and flashlight—all rolled into one. Our objective here is straightforward yet transformative:

1. Understanding Validation: By the end of this chapter, you'll grasp what validation is and isn't. No, it's not about agreeing with everything your partner says or does; it's about understanding their emotional landscape.

2. Why it Matters: You'll explore the psychological nuts and bolts that make validation a crucial relationship skill. Spoiler alert: it's not just about making your partner feel good; it's about creating an emotional sanctuary.

3. Practical Applications: We're not just throwing theory at you; we're giving you a toolkit. You'll learn actionable techniques and exercises to practice validation in your daily interactions.

4. Overcoming Obstacles: Let's face it: validation isn't always easy. We'll delve into common barriers that trip people up and how to navigate them like a pro.

5. Self-Validation: Last but not least, you'll learn the art of self-validation. Because let's be honest, it's not just about understanding your partner; it's about understanding yourself.

What is Validation?

Validation. It's a term we throw around quite casually, isn't it? You might think of it in the context of a parking ticket—something stamped and approved for use. While that's one way to think about it, validation is an entirely different ballgame in relationships.

In the most distilled form, **validation is the acknowledgment and acceptance of another person's thoughts, feelings, sensations, and behaviors as understandable**. It's not about agreeing with them or endorsing their actions; rather, it's about saying, 'Hey, I get where you're coming from, even if I don't necessarily walk the same path.'

Think of it as a high-five to someone's soul—a gesture that says, 'You're seen. You're understood. You're valid.' It's the difference between staring at a painting and saying, 'It's nice,' versus, 'I can sense the emotion in each brushstroke.' The former is a surface-level observation; the latter dives into the essence of the experience.

Validation is a cornerstone in the edifice of emotional intelligence and relational stability. It acts as an emotional mirror, reflecting the thoughts and feelings of the other person in a way that makes them feel understood and supported. In the psychological landscape, it's akin to emotional oxygen—necessary for the survival and flourishing of a healthy relationship.

So, to wrap it up in a neat little bow, validation is your ticket to a deeper, more meaningful connection with your partner and, quite frankly, anyone who's lucky enough to know you.

Types of Validation

So, you've got the basics of validation down. Congratulations! But before you pat yourself on the back and declare yourself the 'Validation Valedictorian,' let's dive deeper. Much like love, chocolate, or a good Netflix series, validation comes in different flavors. Here are the main ones:

Emotional Validation
Remember when you were down in the dumps, someone offered you a listening ear and a shoulder to cry on? That's emotional validation at its finest. This form of validation involves

recognizing and affirming someone's emotional experiences. It's like saying, 'Your feelings matter, and it's okay to feel the way you do.

'It's more than saying, 'I'm sorry you feel that way.' It's about understanding the emotional weight of a situation and offering empathy. Consider it emotional first aid—no Band-Aids required.

Intellectual Validation

Ah, the realm of the thinkers, the debaters, and the occasional over-analyzer (you know who you are!). Intellectual validation is about acknowledging someone's thoughts and ideas. It doesn't mean you have to agree with them, but it's like saying, 'I see the logic in your argument' or 'Your perspective is intriguing.'

This type of validation can be a game-changer in conflicts about decision-making or plans. It's the validation for the mind, where you honor the thought process, even if you don't arrive at the same conclusion.

Situational Validation

Last but not least, let's talk about situational validation. This is where you validate someone's reactions or feelings based on specific circumstances. It's the 'I get why you'd feel that way in this situation' kind of acknowledgment.

Think of it as situational awareness of the emotions. It's especially useful in situations that are emotionally charged or complicated. It helps to de-escalate tension and brings focus back to the issue rather than diverting into emotional alleyways.

And there you have it! The three primary flavors of validation, each with its unique aroma and aftertaste. Next time you find yourself in a validation-worthy situation, you'll have more than one tool in your toolbox. Whether it's an emotional curveball, an intellectual puzzle, or a situational conundrum, you're equipped to handle it.

Psychological Roots

The psychological roots of validation—where science meets the soul, and where therapists get their bread and butter. If validation were a tree, its roots would stretch deep into the fertile soil of psychological theory. Let's put on our Freudian slippers (puns intended, apologies optional) and dig into this fascinating underworld of the mind.

Attachment Theory

First on the list is the ever-popular Attachment Theory, the psychological darling of couples' therapists and self-help books. Proposed by John Bowlby and later popularized by Mary Ainsworth, this theory posits that the bonds formed between children and their primary caregivers lay the foundation for future relationships.

So, how does validation fit in? Think of it as the emotional currency in the attachment economy. In securely attached relationships, validation is like the gold standard—it provides a secure base from which individuals can explore the world and return, knowing that their emotional 'bank' is safe and well-stocked. It's what allows partners to say, 'Go on, chase your dreams, or face your fears. I'll be here, validating your experiences, no matter what.'

In insecure attachments, however, validation is often in short supply, like a rare collectible that everyone wants but few possess. Whether it's the anxious attachment style constantly seeking validation but never feeling it's enough or the avoidant attachment style dodging emotional topics like a ninja, the lack of validation can exacerbate these insecurities.

Cognitive Behavioral Theory (CBT)

Let's pivot to Cognitive Behavioral Theory (CBT), the Swiss Army knife of psychological treatments. CBT focuses on the interplay between thoughts, feelings, and behaviors. In this arena, validation serves as a referee that moderates this complex interplay.

Validating someone's thoughts or feelings doesn't mean you endorse their distorted cognitive schemas or maladaptive behaviors. It means acknowledging their internal experience as real and understandable, giving them the psychological space to question their cognitive distortions. It's like giving someone the emotional 'green light' to explore their thoughts without judgment, making the CBT process more effective.

Mindfulness-Based Approaches

Lastly, let's touch on the Zen cousin in the psychological family—mindfulness-based approaches. Here, validation takes on a meditative quality. It's about being present with what is without trying to change, judge, or solve it. It's the ultimate form of acceptance, where you validate your and your partner's experiences unfolding in the here and now.

And so, dear reader, we come full circle. Whether you're securely attached or working on it or a cognitive behavioral enthusiast or a mindfulness guru, validation is the common thread that weaves through the tapestry of psychological theories. The psychological 'glue' holds the mosaic of human experience together, and by understanding its roots, you're not just a better partner but also a more self-aware individual.

Why Validation Matters

Ah, the million-dollar question: 'Why does validation matter?' You might be tempted to answer, 'Because it feels good, duh!' And while you're not wrong, the significance of validation goes beyond the warm fuzzies it induces. Let's unravel this emotional yarn to see what lies at its core.

Secure Emotional Connection

If relationships were skyscrapers, a secure emotional connection would be the steel framework holding it all together. In this architectural masterpiece, validation plays the role of both the welder and the rivets—it connects and strengthens each emotional beam.

In the realm of emotional security, validation acts like an invisible shield. It doesn't make you invincible, but it certainly makes you resilient. When your thoughts and feelings are validated, you're less likely to be rattled by life's inevitable earthquakes or torn apart by its emotional storms. It's the assurance that no matter how turbulent the external world gets, your internal world has a sanctuary.

So, how does validation accomplish this Herculean feat?

1. **Confidence Booster:** Knowing that your partner understands and accepts your emotional reality boosts your confidence in the relationship and your judgment.

2. **Trust Builder:** Constant validation creates a climate of trust. It's like depositing emotional currency into a trust bank, accruing interest over time.

3. **Conflict Resolver:** Believe it or not, validation is also a secret weapon in resolving conflicts. When both parties feel understood, the battleground shifts from ego to understanding, reducing the emotional casualties on both sides.

4. **Emotional Anchor:** In a world of unpredictability, validation is an emotional anchor. It reassures you that no matter how choppy the waters get, you're not sailing the ship alone.

5. **Intimacy Enhancer:** Last but not least, validation deepens intimacy. It peels away the layers of emotional armor, allowing for a more authentic connection. It's like having a VIP pass to your partner's emotional world, granting you access to corners off-limits to the general public.

Conflict Resolution

Conflicts—the spice of life or the bane of relationships, depending on who you ask. While most of us aren't thrilled at the prospect of a heated disagreement, it's inevitable in any relationship. So, how can validation serve as our trusty shield and sword on this emotional battlefield? Allow me to elucidate.

The Communicative Superpower

Validation is to communication what seasoning is to cooking—it enhances the flavor and makes everything more palatable. When you validate your partner during a disagreement, you're essentially saying, 'I hear you, and your feelings matter.' This simple act can dial down the emotional heat, turning a potential shouting match into a constructive dialogue.

Validation acts as a circuit breaker in heated moments. Imagine you're on the verge of a full-blown argument; your partner says, 'I can see why you'd feel that way.' Suddenly, the steam dissipates, and the pressure lowers. That's validation acting as your emotional thermostat.

The Peace Broker

Conflict often arises from a place of misunderstanding, miscommunication, or downright ignorance. Validation serves as the peace broker in these instances. The diplomatic envoy navigates the treacherous waters of hurt feelings and bruised egos.

Here's how it works:
1. **Neutralizing Negativity:** When you validate your partner's feelings, you neutralize the negative energy that often fuels conflicts. It's akin to dropping a sugar cube into a cup of bitter coffee.

2. **Bridging Divides:** Validation builds bridges over the emotional gaps that disagreements often create. It allows both parties to cross over to a middle ground, where solutions become visible.

3. **Defusing Emotional Bombs:** We all have emotional triggers. Validation acts as a bomb squad that skillfully defuses these triggers, preventing them from blowing up into bigger issues.

4. **Cultivating Empathy:** By validating your partner, you also cultivate empathy within yourself. This helps you to not only understand your partner's point of view but also to articulate your feelings in a more nuanced manner.

5. **Enhancing Emotional Literacy:** Over time, practicing validation can increase both partners' emotional literacy, equipping them with the language and understanding needed to navigate future conflicts with greater finesse.

So, if you've been treating conflicts like an unavoidable natural disaster, think again. With validation in your toolkit, conflicts can transform from destructive tornadoes into constructive winds of change. It's your secret weapon for turning relationship battles into collaborative problem-solving sessions.

Communication Gaps: When Words Fail or Are Misunderstood

Communication gaps—the silent killers of many a promising relationship. They're like the plot holes in an otherwise gripping novel, frustrating and confusing but uncommon. You might think you're saying one thing, but your partner hears something entirely different. Or worse, they hear nothing because your words got lost in translation. Let's uncover why these gaps happen and how validation can be the bridge to better understanding.

The Game of Broken Telephone

Remember that childhood game of broken telephone, where a message gets distorted as it passes from one person to another? Well, relationships often suffer from a grown-up version of this game. Except, the stakes are higher, and the distortions less amusing.

Validation plays the role of a communication 'fixer' in this context. When you validate what your partner is saying—even if you don't fully understand it—you're essentially saying, 'I may not get it completely, but I'm willing to try.' This opens up a space for clarification and minimizes misunderstandings.

The Emotional Filters

We all have emotional filters—previous experiences, current moods, insecurities—that color how we perceive spoken words. These filters can act as smokescreens, distorting the intended meaning of a message. By validating your partner's feelings and perspectives, you can both work to clear away the smoke and see each other more clearly.

The Art of 'Non-Saying'

Sometimes, the most significant communication gaps come from what's not being said. This is where validation becomes a form of emotional telepathy, allowing you to read between the lines and understand the unspoken. For instance, acknowledging that you sense something is off can catalyze open dialogue if your partner seems distant but won't say why.

The Lost-in-Translation Moments

Language is tricky; we've all had 'lost-in-translation' moments. When words fail, validation through actions can speak volumes. A hug, a comforting touch, or even attentive silence can convey what words cannot.

So, if you find yourself in the communication abyss, remember that validation is your lifeline. It's the language of emotional intelligence, a dialect that transcends words and deepens into the heart. Master it, and you'll close the communication gaps and pave the way for a more genuine, understanding relationship.

Emotional Triggers

Ah, emotional triggers—the ghosts of experiences past that love to make unexpected appearances, usually at the most inconvenient times. Like during a heartfelt conversation with your partner when striving for mutual validation. Talk about bad timing, right? But worry not, dear reader, for we are about to embark on a therapeutic ghost hunt.

The Haunting of Past Experiences

When discussing emotional triggers, it's essential to acknowledge that these are often remnants of past experiences or traumas. Think of them as emotional scars that haven't fully healed. They're the landmines in the validation field, ready to explode with the slightest misstep.

Here's the rub:

1. **Baggage Check:** We all bring emotional baggage into relationships. Sometimes, this baggage is packed with past traumas or experiences that make validation challenging.

2. **Defense Mechanisms:** The emotional armor we don for battle. Past experiences often lead to developing defense mechanisms that can act as barriers to validation.

3. **Cycle of Reactivity:** An experience triggers an emotional response, which in turn hampers validation, thus creating a cycle of reactivity. It's like a merry-go-round that nobody enjoys.

The Impact on Validation

So how do these emotional Caspers interfere with validation? They're experts at hijacking conversations and steering them into stormy waters.

1. **Derailing Dialogue:** Emotional triggers can quickly derail a productive dialogue, replacing validation with accusation, blame, or withdrawal.

2. **Selective Hearing:** Triggers often lead to selective hearing, where you're so focused on your emotional response that you miss out on the validating cues from your partner.

3. **Emotional Flooding:** When a trigger hits, it can flood your emotional system, drowning out any attempts at validation.

Exorcising Emotional Ghosts

Enough about the problem; let's talk solutions.

1. **Self-awareness:** Recognizing emotional triggers is the first step in tackling them. Keep an emotional journal to identify patterns.

2. **Time-Outs:** When you feel a trigger activated, take a time-out. It's your emotional pause button.

3. **Safe Spaces:** Create a safe space where you and your partner can openly discuss triggers and work on validating each other despite them.

4. **Professional Help:** Sometimes, the ghosts are too stubborn, and you need a professional exorcist, a therapist, to help you through.

A roadmap for navigating the haunted house of emotional triggers in your quest for validation. Remember, it's not about erasing these triggers but learning to co-exist with them without letting them sabotage your validation efforts. After all, even ghosts need love, right?

Chapter Exercises

Gratitude Mapping

Objective:

The Gratitude Mapping exercise is designed to cultivate appreciation and positive regard within a relationship. By identifying and expressing gratitude for aspects of each other and the relationship, partners can strengthen their emotional connection and enhance mutual understanding.

Materials Needed:

- Paper or notepads.
- Pens or colored markers.
- Optional: stickers or decorative items for a creative touch.

Duration:

20-30 minutes, can be extended as needed.

Instructions:

1. Preparation: Sit together in a comfortable and quiet space. Each partner should have paper/notepad and pens or markers.
2. Introduction to Gratitude Mapping: Explain that the purpose of this exercise is to visually represent things each partner is grateful for in the other person and the relationship. Encourage creativity and honesty in the process.
3. Individual Mapping: Each partner spends some time independently creating their gratitude map. On the map, list or draw things about the other person and the relationship that they are grateful for. This can include qualities, actions, shared experiences, or relationship aspects.
4. Sharing and Discussing Maps: Once both partners have completed their maps, take turns presenting them to each other. Discuss each item on the map, sharing why it's appreciated and how it contributes to the relationship's health and happiness.
5. Reflecting on the Experience: After sharing, reflect together on the experience. Discuss feelings that arose during the exercise and how they might impact your view of each other and the relationship.

6. Planning for Future Actions: Use insights from the exercise to plan how to reinforce these positive aspects. Consider setting goals or intentions based on the elements of gratitude identified in the mapping.

Tips for Success:
- Be as specific as possible when identifying aspects of gratitude.
- Focus on the positive impact of each item listed, reinforcing the emotional bond.
- Keep the maps in a visible place as a reminder of the positive aspects of the relationship.

Conclusion:
Gratitude Mapping is a powerful tool for strengthening relationships by focusing on positive aspects and appreciation. Regularly practicing gratitude can foster a more positive and supportive atmosphere in the relationship, contributing to its overall health and satisfaction.

Emotional Vocabulary Expansion

Objective:

- This exercise aims to enhance emotional awareness and relationship expression by expanding the vocabulary used to describe feelings. This practice helps partners to communicate their emotions more precisely and understand each other's emotional states more deeply.

Materials Needed:
- A comprehensive list of emotional words or a feelings chart (can be found online).
- Notepads and pens.

Duration:
15-20 minutes for each session. This exercise can be repeated regularly.

Instructions:
1. Preparation: Each partner should have access to a comprehensive list of emotional words or a feelings chart. These can be easily found online or created for this purpose. Sit in a comfortable and quiet space with notepads and pens.

2. Familiarization with Emotional Words: Spend a few minutes independently reviewing the list of emotional words. Each partner should mark words that resonate with them or words they find intriguing but rarely use.

3. Sharing Session: Take turns to share a word from the list that resonates with you and explain why. This could relate to a current feeling, a frequent emotion, or an experience. Discuss what the word means to each of you and how it might be used in everyday communication.

4. Reflection on Personal Emotions: Reflect on a recent event or day and describe how you felt using the new words from the list. Be specific, going beyond basic emotions like 'happy' or 'sad.'

5. Expressing Understanding: As one partner shares, the other listens and repeats what they heard, focusing on the emotional words used. This helps in ensuring that the emotions are being understood correctly. Offer validation for the emotions expressed, acknowledging their importance.

6. Role Reversal: Switch roles, allowing the other partner to share their emotions using the new vocabulary.

7. Discussion: Discuss how expanding your emotional vocabulary affects your understanding of each other's feelings. Talk about the importance of accurately expressing emotions in your relationship.

Tips for Success:

- Be open to exploring and accepting a wide range of emotions, even those that may initially feel uncomfortable.
- Encourage each other to express emotions without judgment or criticism.
- Use this expanded vocabulary in daily interactions to become more attuned to each other's emotional states.

Conclusion:

Emotional Vocabulary Expansion is valuable for couples looking to deepen their emotional connection. By enhancing how emotions are communicated, partners can foster greater empathy, understanding, and intimacy. Regular practice of this exercise can significantly improve emotional communication and validation.

Validation in Conflict Resolution

Objective:

To enhance conflict resolution skills by incorporating validation into disagreements. This exercise transforms conflicts into opportunities for deeper understanding and connection, fostering a more compassionate and empathetic approach to resolving issues.

Materials Needed:

- A peaceful, private space for discussion.
  Timer or stopwatch (optional).

Duration:

- This exercise should be used during conflicts, typically 15-30 minutes.

Instructions:

1. Preparing the Environment: Choose a quiet and private area where both partners can speak freely without interruptions. Sit facing each other in a comfortable position, maintaining a non-confrontational posture.
2. Acknowledging the Conflict: Begin by openly acknowledging a disagreement or conflict. Both partners should agree to engage in this exercise to understand and validate rather than win or prove a point.
3. Structured Dialogue: Decide who will speak first. The speaker will express their perspective on the conflict without interruptions. The listener should focus solely on understanding the speaker's point of view, refraining from interjecting, defending, or problem-solving.
4. Active Listening and Validation: Once the speaker has finished, they repeat what they heard, focusing on the emotions and concerns expressed. This is not about agreeing but showing that the speaker's feelings and perspective are heard and acknowledged. Use phrases like 'I understand that you feel...' or 'It sounds like this situation made you feel...'
5. Role Reversal: Switch roles, allowing the other partner to express their perspective while the first speaker listens and then validates.

6. Joint Reflection: After both partners have spoken and listened, reflect on the experience together. Discuss how validation affected the nature of the conflict and whether it led to a deeper understanding of each other's perspectives.
7. Finding Common Ground: Identify any common ground or mutual understanding that emerged during the exercise. Discuss possible solutions or compromises based on this newfound understanding.

Tips for Success:

- Approach the exercise with a genuine willingness to understand your partner's perspective.
- Remember that validating does not mean agreeing with the other person but acknowledging their feelings and points of view.
- Avoid using this time to bring up past grievances. Focus on the current conflict at hand.

Conclusion:

The Validation in Conflict Resolution exercise is a powerful tool for couples to handle disagreements more constructively. By prioritizing understanding and validation over winning an argument, partners can build a stronger, more empathetic foundation for their relationship, turning conflicts into opportunities for growth and deeper connection.

Role-Reversal Exercise

Objective:

To enhance empathy and understanding in the relationship by allowing partners to experience each other's perspectives. This exercise fosters deeper communication and validation by stepping into each other's shoes.

Materials Needed:

- A quiet, comfortable space free from distractions.
- Timer or stopwatch.

Duration:
20-30 minutes, or as needed.

Instructions:
1. Introduction and Setup: Find a calm and comfortable space where both partners can speak without interruptions. Sit facing each other, ensuring a relaxed and open posture.
2. Defining the Roles: Decide who will begin as the 'Speaker' and who will be the 'Listener.' The speaker will share a personal experience or emotion, while the listener will focus on understanding and empathizing with the speaker's perspective.
3. Speaker's Turn: The Speaker shares an experience, thought, or feeling significant to them. It could be a recent event, a persistent concern, or any topic of emotional relevance. The speaker should aim to express their perspective as honestly and openly as possible.
4. Active Listening: The Listener should give their full attention, refraining from interrupting or offering advice. Non-verbal cues like nodding and maintaining eye contact are important to show engagement and understanding.
5. Role-Reversal: After the Speaker has shared, the roles reverse. The listener now becomes the speaker, sharing their own experience or emotion. The original speaker now listens, providing the same attentive and non-judgmental listening.
6. Discussion and Reflection: After both partners have spoken and listened, reflect on the experience. Discuss what it felt like to share and to listen, focusing on any new insights or understandings that emerged from seeing things from the other's perspective.
7. Feedback and Validation: Share feedback on what it felt like to be in the other's role. Discuss how this exercise may affect future communications and the level of empathy in the relationship. Validate each other's feelings and experiences shared during the exercise.
8. Regular Practice: Consider making this exercise a regular part of your communication routine, as it can significantly improve understanding and empathy in the relationship over time.

Tips for Success:
- Approach the exercise with an open mind and heart, ready to truly understand your partner's perspective.

- Avoid minimizing or disputing what your partner shares. The goal is to understand, not to challenge or correct.
- Remember, this exercise is about building empathy and connection, not solving problems or conflicts.

Conclusion:

The Role-Reversal Exercise is an effective tool for building empathy and deepening understanding in a relationship. By experiencing each other's perspectives, partners can develop a more empathetic and validating approach to communication, which is crucial for a healthy and strong relationship.

The Mirror Exercise

Objective:

To improve communication and empathy between partners by practicing accurate listening and reflecting feelings and thoughts, fostering a deeper sense of validation and understanding.

Materials Needed:

- A quiet, comfortable space without distractions.
- Optional: Notepads and pens for each partner.

Duration:

Approximately 20-30 minutes.

Instructions:

1. Setting the Stage: Choose a comfortable, quiet space where both partners can focus without distractions. Sit facing each other in a relaxed posture, maintaining comfortable eye contact.
2. Choosing a Speaker and Listener: Decide who will speak first. The other partner will take on the role of the listener. Switch roles halfway through the exercise.
3. Sharing a Thought or Feeling: The speaker starts by sharing a thought, feeling, or experience. This should be genuine and relevant to their current emotional or recent events. The speaker should be clear and concise, focusing on expressing one main idea or feeling.

4. Active Listening: The listener should give their full attention, avoiding interruptions or preparing a response while the speaker is talking. Non-verbal cues like nodding and maintaining eye contact are important to show engagement.

5. Mirroring Back: Once the speaker is done, the listener mirrors what was said using their own words. The goal is to reflect the essence of the speaker's message and emotions. Phrases like 'What I'm hearing is...', or 'It sounds like you feel...' can be helpful starters.

6. Seeking Clarification: After mirroring, the listener should ask the speaker if they got it right. This can be a simple, 'Did I understand you correctly?' The speaker then has the opportunity to clarify or add more detail if needed.

7. Affirmation and Appreciation: The listener acknowledges the speaker's feelings and thoughts, validating their experience. Express appreciation for sharing, such as, 'Thank you for sharing that with me. It helps me understand how you feel.'

8. Switch Roles: After the first round is complete, switch roles. The previous speaker now becomes the listener and vice versa.

9. Reflection and Discussion: After both partners have had a turn to speak and listen, take some time to reflect on the experience. Discuss how it felt to be heard and understood and how this exercise might impact your daily communication.

Tips for Success:
- Try to keep judgments and solutions out of your reflections. The goal is to understand and validate, not to fix.
- If emotions become intense, take a break and breathe. Remember, this is a practice in understanding, not a debate.
- Practice regularly. The more you practice, the more natural mirroring will become in your daily interactions.

Conclusion:
The Mirror Exercise is a powerful tool for enhancing mutual understanding and validation in a relationship. By practicing active listening and accurate reflection, partners can develop a deeper empathy and appreciation for each other's perspectives, strengthening their emotional connection.

Intimacy and Romance

Intimacy and romance are two aspects of human relationships that are often intertwined but can also be experienced independently. While intimacy refers to the emotional and physical closeness between two individuals, romance involves the feelings of love and attraction associated with a romantic relationship. Both intimacy and romance play important roles in our lives, influencing our emotional well-being and quality of life. In this chapter, we will explore the concepts of intimacy and romance in greater detail, examining their psychological, social, and cultural dimensions.

Intimacy can be described as the ability to share one's deepest thoughts, feelings, and experiences with another person. It involves a sense of emotional vulnerability and the willingness to open up and be honest with someone else. Also, it can be experienced in many different types of relationships, including friendships, familial relationships, and romantic partnerships. In romantic relationships, intimacy is often associated with physical closeness, such as hugging, kissing, and sexual activity. However, emotional intimacy is equally important and involves sharing one's innermost thoughts and feelings with a partner without fear of judgment or rejection.

One of the most significant benefits of intimacy is that it can promote feelings of happiness, contentment, and fulfillment in our lives. When we feel connected to others deeply emotionally, we experience a sense of belonging and purpose that can enhance our overall well-being. Intimacy can also help us feel more confident and secure in ourselves, allowing us to share our strengths and weaknesses with another person who accepts and supports us.

However, intimacy can also be challenging, particularly in our fast-paced and often disconnected modern world. Individuals may struggle to connect with others deeply due to past traumas, fears of vulnerability, or simply a lack of social skills. Some people may also struggle with intimacy in romantic relationships due to past experiences of heartbreak or betrayal. In these cases, it can be helpful to seek the assistance of a mental health professional or relationship counselor who can provide guidance and support in developing healthy intimacy skills.

On the other hand, romance is a distinct aspect of human relationships that involves feelings of love, attraction, and desire. While intimacy can exist in platonic relationships, romance is typically reserved for romantic partnerships. Romance involves a variety of emotions, including infatuation, passion, and affection. Moreover, it can be experienced in different ways, for example, through physical touch, verbal expressions of love, and acts of kindness and affection.

Like intimacy, romance is essential in our lives, contributing to our happiness. Romantic relationships can provide companionship, support, and love that can enhance our lives in many ways. In addition, research has shown that people who are in happy, committed relationships tend to experience better mental and physical health outcomes than those who are single or in unhappy relationships.

And just like intimacy, it can also be hard to achieve, particularly in a world where social norms and expectations can sometimes pressure individuals to conform to certain relationship ideals. For example, there may be pressure to find a partner who meets specific physical or social criteria or follows traditional gender roles. These expectations can create stress and anxiety for individuals who do not meet these standards and may lead to feelings of loneliness and isolation.

One of the most significant challenges of romance is navigating the complexities of human attraction and desire. While physical attraction is often a key component of romantic relationships, it can also be a source of confusion and frustration. Many people struggle with feelings of attraction to individuals who may not be a good match for them in other ways, such as personality or values. Others may struggle with balancing their desire for physical intimacy with their need for emotional connection and trust.

Lack of intimacy and romance in a relationship can lead to a variety of issues, both emotional and physical. Here are some of the common issues that may arise:

Emotional distance: Emotional distance can occur when there is a lack of intimacy and romance in a relationship. This means that partners may feel disconnected or detached from each other, leading to feelings of loneliness, isolation, and dissatisfaction.

Decreased satisfaction: Without intimacy and romance, partners may feel less satisfied with their relationship. They start to feel unfulfilled, unappreciated, or neglected, which leads to resentment and frustration.

Decreased attraction: Intimacy and romance are important factors in attraction between partners. When these aspects are lacking, partners may feel less attracted to each other, leading to a decreased desire for physical intimacy and potentially leading to infidelity.

Stress and anxiety: The absence of intimacy and romance in a relationship can create stress and anxiety for partners. They may worry about the state of their relationship, feel insecure about their partner's feelings, or feel overwhelmed by the effort required to improve the relationship.

Physical health issues: Lack of intimacy and romance can also lead to physical health issues. For example, individuals may experience increased stress levels, which can lead to high blood pressure, heart disease, and other health problems.

Mental health issues: A lack of intimacy and romance can also lead to mental health issues, such as depression and anxiety. Partners may feel hopeless or desperate about their relationship, leading to sadness and distress.

Infertility: In some cases, a lack of intimacy and romance can lead to infertility. It can occur when partners are not having regular sexual intercourse, which leads to decreased fertility over time.

A lack of intimacy and romance can lead to various negative consequences for partners. Therefore, it is important to address these issues early in the relationship and work to improve intimacy and romance to prevent these negative outcomes. To do that, you need to learn the concepts of intimacy and apply different techniques to maintain a healthy intimacy level.

Types of intimacy in a healthy relationship

Emotional intimacy

Emotional intimacy in a relationship refers to the closeness, trust, and vulnerability of two individuals. It is the ability to be open and honest with your partner about your deepest thoughts, feelings, fears, and desires and to feel accepted and understood by them.

Emotional intimacy involves sharing your innermost self with your partner, knowing they will listen to you without judgment, and responding with empathy and compassion. It involves feeling safe enough to share your vulnerabilities and being able to support your partner in the same way.

When partners have emotional intimacy, they feel connected deeply, creating a sense of closeness and security. Therefore, emotional intimacy is essential for a healthy relationship, as it allows partners to develop trust, build a strong bond, and feel fulfilled.

Intellectual intimacy

Intellectual intimacy in a relationship refers to the ability of two individuals to share their thoughts, ideas, and perspectives in a profound and meaningful way. It involves engaging in conversations that challenge and stimulate each other's minds and exploring new ideas and concepts together.

Intellectual intimacy is not just about having similar interests or being knowledgeable about the same topics but rather about understanding and respecting each other's intellectual abilities and perspectives. It involves expressing oneself freely without fear of being judged and being open to learning from one's partner.

When partners have intellectual intimacy, they can engage in stimulating conversations and debates that lead to personal growth and mutual understanding. They can learn from each other's experiences and perspectives and share a mutual respect for intellect. This intimacy can enhance the emotional connection between partners as they learn to appreciate and value each other's unique perspectives and insights.

Physical intimacy

Physical intimacy in a relationship refers to the physical closeness and connection between partners. It can involve a range of physical acts, including holding hands, hugging, kissing, cuddling, and sexual activity.

Physical intimacy is an important aspect of a healthy romantic relationship, as it allows partners to express their love and affection for each other tangibly. In addition, it can create a sense of intimacy and closeness between partners and help build and maintain emotional connections.

Physical intimacy can also provide many health benefits, both physical and emotional. For example, it can release feel-good hormones like oxytocin, reduce stress levels, and boost immune function. It can also enhance emotional well-being and promote feelings of happiness and satisfaction.

However, it's important to note that physical intimacy should always be consensual and respectful. It's essential to communicate openly with your partner about your boundaries and preferences and prioritize each other's comfort and safety.

Gottman's approach to maintaining romance

The Gottman Method is a couples therapy approach developed by Drs. John and Julie Gottman. It is a research-based approach that focuses on improving communication, understanding, and the overall quality of the relationship. The method is designed to help couples strengthen their relationship by addressing issues related to emotional intimacy, conflict resolution, and relationship building.

The Gottman Method is based on over four decades of research and has been extensively tested and refined. The approach focuses on seven essential principles for a healthy and successful relationship. These principles include building love maps, nurturing fondness and admiration, turning toward each other instead of away, having a positive perspective, managing conflict, making life dreams come true, and creating shared meaning.

The first principle of the Gottman Method is building love maps. It involves knowing each other's world, including likes, dislikes, and life goals. Couples can build a stronger bond by creating a strong foundation of understanding and knowing each other.

The second principle is nurturing fondness and admiration. It involves expressing appreciation and affection toward each other, focusing on the positive aspects of the relationship, and building a sense of fondness and affection.

The third principle is turning toward each other instead of away, which means being responsive to each other's needs, supporting each other emotionally, and being there for one's partner in times of need.

The fourth principle is the positive perspective. This principle involves seeing the best in each other and the relationship, even during conflict or stress.

The fifth principle is managing conflict. This principle entails learning to communicate effectively, listening to each other's concerns, and finding ways to resolve conflict healthily and constructively.

The sixth principle is making life's dreams come true. It involves supporting each other's goals and aspirations and working together to achieve them.

The seventh principle is creating shared meaning. This principle involves building a sense of purpose and meaning in the relationship by creating traditions and rituals that strengthen the bond between partners.

The Gottman Method uses various techniques and exercises to help couples strengthen their relationship. These include learning effective communication skills, identifying and changing negative relationship patterns, and building intimacy and connection.

One of the key features of the Gottman Method is the use of assessments to help couples identify areas of strength and areas for improvement. These assessments include the Relationship Checkup, which helps couples identify the areas of their relationship that need attention, and the Love Maps Card Deck, which helps couples deepen their understanding of each other.

The Gottman Method is a comprehensive approach to couples therapy that emphasizes building a strong foundation of understanding, communication, and connection. It is grounded in extensive research and is effective in helping couples improve their relationship satisfaction and overall well-being.

To delve deeper into the techniques that Gottman could recommend, here are a few activities to remember to keep intimacy and romance alive.

The importance of rituals and routines

Rituals and routines play an essential role in maintaining healthy and happy relationships. They provide a sense of stability, comfort, and predictability that can help couples navigate the ups and downs of life together. Here are some reasons why rituals and routines are important in relationships:

Creating a sense of connection: Rituals and routines can create a deeper connection and intimacy between partners. Whether having a weekly date night or a morning coffee together, these activities can help couples bond and feel more connected.

Providing a sense of security: In a world that is often unpredictable and chaotic, rituals and routines can provide a sense of security and stability for couples. Knowing they have a set time to connect and spend together can be comforting and reassuring.

Promoting positive communication: Rituals and routines allow positive communication between partners. Whether discussing their day over dinner or sharing their thoughts and feelings during a morning walk, these activities can help couples communicate healthily and constructively.

Building a shared history: Rituals and routines can create a sense of shared history and memories between partners. Whether it's a yearly vacation or a holiday tradition, these activities can create a sense of continuity and shared experiences that can strengthen the relationship.

Fostering personal growth: Rituals and routines can also provide personal growth and development opportunities. Whether working out or taking a class together, these activities can help couples grow and learn, leading to a deeper sense of connection and intimacy.

Overall, rituals and routines can be an essential part of maintaining a healthy and happy relationship. They provide a sense of connection, security, and intimacy between partners and can help couples navigate the ups and downs of life together. Here are some examples of activities you can do together.

Regular date nights

Regular date nights are important for couples for several reasons:

Rekindling Romance: Date nights allow couples to rekindle the romance and intimacy in their relationship. They are times to focus on each other and to remind each other why you fell in love in the first place.

Quality Time: In today's fast-paced world, couples often juggle work, family, and other responsibilities, leaving little time for each other. Date nights allow couples to spend quality time together without distractions, providing an opportunity to deepen their connection.

Communication: Date nights are an excellent opportunity for couples to communicate and connect. They allow them to share their thoughts, feelings, and experiences in a relaxed and comfortable setting, helping to strengthen their emotional bond.

Variety and Fun: Regular date nights allow couples to try new things and have fun together. It could be trying a new restaurant, taking a cooking class, or attending a concert. Whatever activity you choose would help keep the relationship fresh and exciting.

Stress Relief: Date nights provide a break from the stresses of everyday life. They allow couples to step away from their daily responsibilities and focus on themselves, which can help reduce stress and improve mental health.

Commitment: Scheduling regular date nights shows a commitment to the relationship. It shows that both partners are willing to make time for each other and prioritize their relationship, which can help strengthen their bond.

Regular date nights are important for maintaining a healthy and happy relationship. It allows couples to rekindle romance, communicate, have fun, relieve stress, and show commitment. Couples can deepen their connection and strengthen their relationship by setting aside time for regular date nights.

Expressing appreciation and gratitude daily

Expressing appreciation and gratitude daily in a relationship is a powerful way to strengthen the bond between partners and cultivate a more positive and loving atmosphere. Here are some benefits of expressing appreciation and gratitude in a relationship:

Promotes positivity: Expressing appreciation and gratitude regularly promotes a more positive and loving atmosphere in the relationship. It helps to shift the focus away from negative aspects and towards the positive aspects of the relationship.

Increases intimacy: Regularly expressing appreciation and gratitude helps to build intimacy between partners. It creates a safe and comfortable environment where both partners feel valued and appreciated, which helps to deepen their emotional connection.

Boosts self-esteem: When partners express appreciation and gratitude for each other, it can boost their self-esteem and self-worth. It creates a sense of validation and appreciation, motivating positive behaviors and actions.

Reduces stress: Expressing appreciation and gratitude can help reduce relationship stress. It helps to create a more relaxed and positive environment, which helps alleviate stress and tension.

Strengthens the relationship: Regularly expressing appreciation and gratitude can help strengthen the relationship over time. It creates a positive feedback loop where partners feel appreciated and valued, motivating them to continue positive behaviors and actions towards each other.

Some simple ways to express appreciation and gratitude daily in a relationship include:

- Saying "thank you" for the little things your partner does for you
- Giving your partner a compliment
- Writing a note of appreciation or gratitude
- Verbally expressing your appreciation and gratitude for your partner's qualities, actions, and efforts
- Doing something special or thoughtful for your partner

Expressing daily appreciation and gratitude in a relationship is a simple yet powerful way to strengthen the bond between partners, promote positivity, increase intimacy, boost self-esteem, reduce stress, and strengthen the overall relationship.

The role of small gestures and acts of service

Small gestures and acts of service can play a vital role in maintaining a strong, healthy, and fulfilling bond between partners. These actions help demonstrate love, appreciation, and care for one another daily.

Some examples of small gestures in a relationship include leaving a love note for your partner, making their favorite breakfast in bed, bringing them a cup of tea or coffee in the morning, or simply giving them a warm hug or kiss.

Acts of service can also be a powerful way to show love and support in a relationship. They include doing the dishes or laundry, running errands, cooking dinner, or helping with a project or task your partner struggles with.

These small gestures and acts of service strengthen the emotional connection between partners, promote a sense of teamwork and collaboration, and create a positive, supportive environment for both individuals in the relationship.

The concept of the "6-second kiss" for daily connection

The "6-second kiss" is a simple but powerful concept that can help couples maintain a strong emotional connection. The idea is to take six seconds to give your partner a deep, meaningful kiss each day without any distractions or interruptions.

Research has shown that physical touch, like kissing, can release feel-good hormones like oxytocin and dopamine, which help reduce stress, boost mood, and improve overall well-being. By taking just six seconds to connect with your partner, you can help reinforce the emotional bond between you and your partner and create a sense of intimacy and closeness.

The "6-second kiss" is also a way to prioritize your relationship amid busy, stressful schedules. Connecting with your partner can show them they are a priority in your life and help strengthen your commitment to one another.

EFT's perspective on emotional and physical intimacy

Emotion-focused therapy (EFT) is an approach to psychotherapy based on the idea that emotions are a primary source of information about ourselves and our experiences. As a result, they play a central role in our relationships and mental health. EFT was developed in the 1980s by Dr. Leslie Greenberg and Dr. Sue Johnson and has since been used to treat a wide range of emotional and relational issues.

EFT aims to help individuals and couples better understand and manage their emotions and use them to guide healing and growth. This method is practiced through a collaborative and empathic therapeutic relationship, where the therapist helps the client identify and express their emotions and explore the underlying thoughts, beliefs, and behaviors that may contribute to their emotional struggles.

Here are some concepts that EFT recommends to help build a more stable relationship:

Understanding attachment needs and fears

Attachment needs and fears are related to how we form and maintain close relationships with others, and they can play a significant role in our emotional well-being.

Attachment needs refer to the basic human desire to feel loved, secure, and connected to others. These needs are rooted in early childhood experiences and are shaped by our interactions with primary caregivers. They include feeling valued and respected, having a sense of trust and safety, and feeling emotionally connected to others.

On the other hand, attachment fears are the negative emotions and behaviors that arise when these needs are unmet. Some common attachment fears include fear of abandonment, rejection, or loss of control. These fears can lead to negative behaviors like clinginess, jealousy, or emotional withdrawal.

Understanding our attachment needs and fears can be a valuable tool for promoting healthy relationships and emotional well-being. By identifying our attachment needs, we can ensure they are met in our relationships, such as communicating openly and honestly with our partners and setting healthy boundaries. Likewise, by recognizing our attachment fears, we can overcome them by challenging negative self-talk or seeking therapy to address deeper emotional wounds.

Cultivating a deeper understanding of our attachment needs and fears can build stronger, more fulfilling relationships and lead emotionally satisfying lives.

Creating a secure base for exploring vulnerability and intimacy

Creating a secure base for exploring vulnerability and intimacy is essential for building strong, healthy relationships. A secure base is a foundation of trust, safety, and support that allows individuals to feel comfortable being vulnerable and opening up emotionally to their partners.

To create a secure base, it is important to establish clear and healthy communication with your partner, which involves being open and honest about your needs and desires and actively listening to and validating your partner's feelings and concerns.

Establishing boundaries and guidelines for how you will interact is important, such as setting aside dedicated time to connect and being mindful of each other's emotional needs.

Another key component of creating a secure base is building a foundation of mutual respect and trust. This means being consistent in your actions and words and showing that you can be relied upon to provide emotional support and comfort.

Finally, it is important to remember that creating a secure base for exploring vulnerability and intimacy is an ongoing process that requires continual effort and attention. It may involve taking risks and stepping outside of your comfort zone, but the rewards of a strong and fulfilling relationship can be well worth the effort.

Identifying and addressing blocks to intimacy

Intimacy is essential to any healthy relationship, but sometimes, blocks or barriers may prevent individuals from experiencing true intimacy with their partner. These blocks can take many forms, including physical, emotional, mental, or spiritual barriers. Here are some common blocks to intimacy and ways to address them:

Fear of vulnerability: Being vulnerable and sharing our deepest thoughts and feelings with someone else can be scary, especially if we've been hurt. To overcome this block, it's important to communicate openly and honestly with your partner about your fears and to work together to build a safe and trusting environment.

Negative self-talk: Negative self-talk and self-doubt can prevent individuals from feeling confident and comfortable in their skin, impacting their ability to connect intimately with their partner. Addressing negative self-talk may involve identifying and challenging negative beliefs, practicing self-compassion, and building self-confidence.

Lack of communication: A lack of communication can prevent individuals from building a deeper connection with their partner. It's important to set aside time to talk openly and honestly with your partner and actively listen and respond to their needs and concerns.

Trauma: Past trauma can create emotional blocks that prevent individuals from fully connecting with their partners. In these cases, seeking therapy or other professional support may be helpful to work through past trauma and heal from emotional wounds.

Busy schedules and distractions: Busy schedules and distractions can prevent individuals from making time for intimacy with their partner. It's important to prioritize intimacy and make time for it in your schedule, even if it means cutting back on other activities.

Sexual difficulties: Sexual difficulties, such as performance anxiety or lack of desire, can create barriers to intimacy. It's important to communicate openly with your partner about any sexual difficulties and to seek out professional support if needed.

Individuals and couples can create a more intimate and fulfilling relationship by identifying and addressing blocks to intimacy. It's important to approach these barriers with compassion and a willingness to work together to create a safe and loving environment for emotional connection.

Chapter Exercises

Exercise: "Intimate Questions"

Introduction

Are your conversations with your partner starting to feel like you're both characters in a poorly written-sitcom? Enough of the 'How was your day?' and 'What's for dinner?' chatter. Let's delve into the delicious depths of each other's souls. Ready for a conversation that can be as enlightening as it is titillating? Let's play 20 questions—maybe just six, but who's counting?

Objective

This intimate inquiry aims to crack open the vault of emotional and, dare we say, sexual treasures that lie within each of you. This isn't just chit-chat; this is about laying bare your innermost fears, desires, and maybe even some fantasies. Fasten your seatbelts; it's going to be an exhilarating ride.

Materials Needed

- A cozy, intimate setting (candlelight optional but highly recommended)
- A sense of adventure and a dash of courage

Note to the Couple

This is your chance to go spelunking in the caverns of each other's minds (and maybe hearts and other parts?). But remember, you're both explorers on this journey—so no judgment is allowed. Let curiosity be your guide and vulnerability your compass.

Detailed Steps

Step 1: Setting the Stage

Example: Dim the lights, pour wine, and put on mood music. Let Barry White or Norah Jones serenade you into the right state of mind.

First, create the right atmosphere. This is not a Q&A session; think of it as a verbal tango.

Step 2: The Questions Unveiled

Example: 'What is your most secret desire?' or 'What's a fantasy you've never shared?'

- Each partner should take a moment to conjure up three questions daring enough to ignite sparks but respectful enough not to start a wildfire.

Step 3: The Inquisition Begins

Example: Asking, 'What's the most adventurous thing you've ever wanted to do in bed?'

- Take turns asking your questions. Listen to your partner's answer as if it's sacred magic—because it is.

Step 4: The Afterglow

Example: Realizing that you both share a hidden desire to go on a romantic getaway to Paris.

- Once all questions have been asked and answered, bask in the afterglow of newfound understanding and, quite possibly, excitement.

Tips and Notes

1. Spice, Not Fire: Aim for provocative but not offensive questions.
2. Consent is King (and Queen): Make sure you are comfortable diving into these intimate waters.

Keep the Mystery: Remember, this exercise isn't about spilling all your beans—just a few compelling ones.

Activity: "Sensual Massage Night (Rubbing the Right Way)"

Introduction

Touch is a powerful language that conveys love, care, and intimacy. In this activity, you will explore the sensual art of massage, a beautiful way to connect with your partner physically. So grab some aromatic oils and prepare for an evening of relaxation and intimacy.

Objective

To deepen your physical and emotional connection through the intimate act of giving and receiving massages.

Materials Needed
- Aromatic massage oils
- Soft towels or a comfortable mat
- Candles or dim lighting
- Calming background music

Note to the Couple
Prepare to transcend the ordinary as you communicate with your hands and listen with your skin. This isn't just a massage; it's a tactile dialogue between you and your partner.

Detailed Steps
Step 1: Set the Atmosphere
Example: Light some scented candles and play soft instrumental music.
- Create a calming atmosphere that invites relaxation and intimacy. This means soft lighting, soothing music, and a comfortable surface.

Step 2: Choose Your Oils
Example: Opt for lavender oil for relaxation or peppermint oil for a stimulating effect.
- Pick aromatic oils that both of you find pleasing. Different oils offer different benefits, so choose ones that suit your mood.

Step 3: Learn Basic Techniques
Example: Check out a few YouTube tutorials on basic massage techniques.
- Before diving in, watching some instructional videos to learn basic massage techniques might be helpful. This will make the experience more enjoyable for both the giver and the receiver.

Step 4: The Sensual Exchange
Example: Start with a shoulder massage and gradually work your way down.
- Now comes the fun part. Take turns giving each other massages. Focus on tense areas and sync your movements with your partner's breath.

Tips and Notes

1. Take Your Time: This is not a race; let each stroke be a prolonged expression of your affection.
2. Communicate: Ask your partner about the pressure and if there are specific areas they'd like you to focus on.
3. Enjoy the Silence: While the conversation is good, cherish the quiet moments you can connect without words.

Exercise: "Romantic Timeline"

Introduction

In the tapestry of a relationship, certain threads stand out—these moments of intense romance elevate your connection and become cherished memories. A 'Romantic Timeline' allows you to revisit these milestones, celebrate your journey together, and perhaps even rekindle some of that initial magic.

Objective

This exercise aims to help you and your partner relive and celebrate the significant romantic milestones in your relationship. By creating a physical or mental timeline, you can gain perspective on how far you've come, your shared experiences, and the romantic energy that has fueled your relationship.

Duration

45-60 minutes

Materials Needed

*   Pen and paper or a digital platform like a shared document
*   Photos or keepsakes related to significant romantic events (optional)

Pre-Exercise Note

The 'Romantic Timeline' exercise offers couples a chance to reflect on the evolution of their relationship. It can be particularly useful for couples who feel stuck in a routine or are experiencing a romantic slump. See this as more than a trip down memory lane; it's an opportunity to understand the elements contributing to your romantic connection.

Detailed Steps

Step 1: Gather Materials

Choose a medium for your timeline—pen and paper for something tangible or a digital platform. Collect photos or keepsakes corresponding to significant romantic moments you'd like to include.

Step 2: Plotting the Timeline

Example: Mark your first kiss, the day you exchanged 'I love yous,' and your most memorable date.

- Begin by plotting the major romantic milestones in your relationship.
- Each partner should take turns adding events to the timeline.

Step 3: Adding Details

Example: Add little notes or symbols to signify your emotions—like a heart for love or a star for a particularly magical moment.

- Add details to each event on the timeline. This could be a few sentences about your feelings, what made it special, or even a relevant photo.

Step 4: Reflection and Discussion

Example: Reflect on how you both have grown in your ability to love and be loved. What patterns do you see?

- Take some time to reflect on your timeline. Look for patterns, significant gaps, or periods of intense romantic activity.
- Discuss these observations with your partner.

Step 5: Future Additions

Example: Maybe you've always wanted to dance under the stars; add this to your plans.

- As a final step, discuss and add any future romantic events or experiences you both look forward to.

Tips and Notes
1. Be Present: This is a time for connection; try to minimize distractions.
2. Be Honest but Tactful: Your partner's significant moments may differ from yours.
3. Embrace these differences rather than debate them.
4. Keep it Alive: Consider revisiting your Romantic Timeline annually or during significant life changes to update it and keep your romantic connection strong.

Exercise: "Romantic Date Night (Breaking the Monotony, One Date at a Time)"

Introduction
Let's face it: the 'Netflix and chill' routine is getting stale. It's time to crank up the romance and break the everyday monotony. This exercise is your ticket to rekindling that spark through an extraordinary date night. Ready to trade your sweatpants for some adventure?

Objective
The goal here isn't just to have a 'good time' but a 'mind-blowingly awesome time.' We're talking about a date night that revives the thrill, the romance, and maybe even the butterflies.

Materials Needed
- A dash of imagination
- A sprinkle of willingness to try something new
- Optional: A 'Do Not Disturb' sign for your front door

Note to the Couple
This is not a drill; this is a romantic emergency intervention! Your mission is to step outside your comfort zone and into a world of exciting possibilities.

Detailed Steps
Step 1: Brainstorm Unique Date Ideas
Example: How about a cooking class where you both learn to make sushi?

- Both of you should brainstorm unique, out-of-the-box date ideas. Think skydiving, treasure hunts, or even a night at a museum.

Step 2: Plan Your Adventure

Example: If you opt for a hot air balloon ride, book the tickets, set the date, and make any necessary arrangements.

- Once you've agreed on a date idea, take the steps to make it happen. This could involve bookings, reservations, or buying special items.

Step 3: The Big Night

Example: Dress up, show up, and let the adventure unfold.

- On the day of your date, could you make an effort to make it special? Dress up, be present, and let go of any expectations.

Step 4: Relive the Magic

Example: Spend the next day looking through photos or discussing your favorite moments.

- After your date, take some time to relive the experience. What did you enjoy the most? What would you do differently next time?

Tips and Notes

1. Go Big or Home: This is not the time to play it safe. Choose an idea that makes both of you a little excited and nervous.
2. Document the Fun: Take pictures or videos to capture the magic.
3. Leave Room for Spontaneity: While planning is good, leave some room for unexpected adventures.

Fun Date Night Ideas

1. Stargazing from a secluded spot.
2. A 'staycation' at a fancy hotel in your city.
3. A cooking challenge where each of you makes a surprise dish for the other.
4. An 'around-the-world' dining experience: appetizers, main course, and dessert, each from a different cuisine.
5. A sunrise hike followed by a cozy breakfast.
6. A themed movie night with costumes and snacks to match.

7. A 'bucket list' day where you each get to do something you've always wanted.
8. A dance class to learn a style neither of you has tried before.
9. A DIY paint-and-sip night at home.
10. A 'mystery date' where each person plays a part of the date, but it's a surprise for the other.

Exercise: "Role Reversal"

Introduction

Ever looked at your partner and thought, 'I wonder what it's like to be you for a day?' No, we're not venturing into sci-fi territory; we're diving into a role reversal exercise! This playful yet enlightening activity allows you to experience a day in your partner's shoes. Get ready for some eye-opening and possibly hilarious revelations.

Objective

The objective is to understand better your partner's daily life, responsibilities, and challenges. This isn't just empathy; this is empathy on steroids.

Materials Needed

- A sense of humor (mandatory)
- Willingness to be a good sport (also mandatory)
- A day where both of you are free to swap roles (highly recommended)

Note to the Couple

This exercise is about more than just trading places; it's about trading perspectives. While it's all in good fun, the insights you gain could be invaluable for your relationship.

Detailed Steps

Step 1: Define the Roles

Example: If one usually handles cooking and the other handles finances, jot that down.

- Each of you should list the daily responsibilities or roles you typically assume. Make it detailed but not overwhelming.

Step 2: The Swap
Example: Switching who makes the morning coffee and who walks the dog.
- Once you have your lists, swap them. For one day, each of you will take on the roles and responsibilities of the other.

Step 3: Live It Up (or Down)
Example: Going through the day juggling tasks that are usually not in your domain.
- Go through the day performing each other's tasks. Feel free to call or text if you run into any 'How do I do this?' moments.

Step 4: Debrief and Revelations
Example: Realizing that making dinner isn't as easy as it looks.
- Discuss your experiences. What surprised you? What did you find challenging or enlightening?

Tips and Notes
1. Keep It Light: This exercise can be fun but also eye-opening. Could you take it in stride?
2. Don't Cheat: The point is to try to fulfill each other's roles, not to prove who's better at what.
3. Reflect: Use this experience as a mirror to see your partner's life and reflect on your own.

Exercise: "Affectionate Texting" (or How to Make Emojis Work for Your Love Life)

Introduction
Did you ever send a text and then wait anxiously, staring at those dreaded three dots, only to get a 'K' in return? We've all been there. But what if I told you that your phone, that same device you use to order pizza, can also deliver slices of affection? Welcome to the world of 'Affectionate Texting,' where we turn that soulless screen into a love letter, one emoji at a time.

Objective

Your mission, should you accept it, is to rekindle the flames of affection through the art of texting. You'll send your partner thoughtful, affectionate, and (hopefully) typo-free messages. The goal? To add a sprinkle of intimacy to the pixelated words on your screen.

Materials Needed

- A smartphone (Sorry, carrier pigeons won't work here.)
- A splash of creativity and a handful of emojis (or emoticons if you're old school)

Pre-Exercise Note

Prepare to navigate the digital landscape of love. This exercise isn't just about hitting 'send'; it's about sending ripples through the heart.

Detailed Steps

Step 1: Mastering the Art of Textual Affection

Example: Swap 'WYD?' with 'Thinking of you. How's your day going?'

- Each partner should brainstorm affectionate messages beyond the usual 'Hey' or 'What's up?' Let's elevate texting to an art form!

Step 2: Unleashing the Texts (The Good Kind)

Example: 'Missing you. I wish you were here. 🌹' Ah, now we're talking!

- Ready, set, text! Start by sending one affectionate text a day. Don't overthink it; let spontaneity take the wheel.

Step 3: The Emoji Response Meter

Example: If a '🖤' is responded to with a '😊,' you're golden. If it's a '👎,' we might need to talk.

- Notice how your partner reacts. No, you don't need to hold a post-text debriefing, but a little acknowledgment never hurt anyone.

Step 4: The Textual Analysis (The Fun Kind)

Example: Realize that the '🌹' emojis have been a hit and decide to keep the floral theme going.

- After a week of turning the digital airwaves into your love song, sit down to discuss the hits and misses. Keep what works, tweak what doesn't.

Tips and Notes

1. Be Yourself: If 'I pine for thee' isn't your style, stick to what feels natural. Just make it heartfelt.
2. Quality Over Quantity: One 'I love you' can outweigh a dozen 'LOLs.'
3. When in Doubt, Emoji It Out: Sometimes a picture—or an emoji—is worth a thousand words.

Exercise: "Mindful Touching"

Introduction

Touch is a language that conveys love, comfort, and support without uttering a single word. Yet, in the hustle and bustle of daily life, the quality of touch often gets overlooked. 'Mindful Touching' aims to bring intentionality and awareness into your physical interactions with your partner.

Objective

This exercise focuses on cultivating physical intimacy through the practice of mindfulness. You and your partner will engage in a touching exercise, paying close attention to the sensations and emotions that arise. The goal is to deepen your physical connection while also being fully present in the moment.

Duration

15-20 minutes

Materials Needed

- A quiet, comfortable space free from distractions
- Optional: Soft background music or nature sounds

Pre-Exercise Note

Mindful Touching can be an incredibly intimate experience and may bring up intense emotions for some couples. It's essential to create a safe and comfortable environment.

Ensure both partners are open to this level of physical intimacy and understand the exercise's intention.

Detailed Steps
Step 1: Preparing the Space
Choose a quiet room or area where you both can sit comfortably. If you prefer, you can put on some soft background music.

Step 2: Setting Intentions
Example: Your intention could be to deepen your emotional connection through touch.
- Before you begin, each partner should silently set an intention for this exercise.
- Share your intentions.

Step 3: The Touching Exercise
Example: One partner can touch the other's arm, focusing on the texture of the skin, the warmth, and any sensations that arise.
- Sit facing each other and decide who will be the 'toucher' first.
- The 'toucher' will gently touch their partner's hand, arm, or any non-sensitive area, focusing entirely on the sensation of touch.
- After 2-5 minutes, switch roles.

Step 4: Reflection and Sharing
Example: You might have felt a sense of peace, love, or vulnerability while touching or being touched.
- Take turns sharing your experiences, sensations, and any emotions that arose.

Tips and Notes
1. Remain Open: This is an exercise in vulnerability. Try to remain open to both giving and receiving touch.
2. No Judgement: The goal is not to analyze your feelings but to experience them fully.
3. Adapt as Needed: If you or your partner are uncomfortable with any aspect of the exercise, feel free to adapt it to suit your boundaries.

Exercise: "Appreciation Journal (Because Love Should Be More Than Just a Four-Letter Word)"

Introduction

In the hustle and bustle of life, it's easy to overlook the little things that make your relationship special. Enter the Appreciation Journal—a dedicated space to recognize and celebrate what you love about each other. Think of it as a 'love bank' where deposits always appreciate!

Objective

The goal is to cultivate a habit of recognizing and documenting the positive aspects of your relationship. This will serve as a tangible reminder of your love, especially when you need it the most.

Materials Needed
- A beautiful journal that you both like
- Pens that bring you joy (yes, the pen type can make a difference!)
- A few quiet moments each day

Note to the Couple

This isn't your average diary; it's a treasure chest where you store nuggets of love and appreciation. So, be generous with your entries. The more you deposit, the richer your emotional wealth.

Detailed Steps

Step 1: Choose Your Journal

Example: A leather-bound journal that smells of nostalgia or a quirky notebook that brings a smile to your face.
- Start by choosing a journal that resonates with both of you. It should be something you'll be excited to write in.

Step 2: Set a Routine

Example: Decide to make entries every Sunday evening to reflect the past week.
- Establish a routine for when and how often you'll make entries. Consistency is key, whether daily, weekly, or even monthly.

Step 3: Make Your First Entries

Example: Write about how your partner's laughter fills the room with warmth.

- Begin with your first entries. Write about something you appreciate about your partner, no matter how small. It could be an action, a character trait, or a memorable moment.

Step 4: Keep It Going

Example: Don't just stop at one entry. Make it a point to keep adding to the journal.

- Continue to add to the journal as per your routine. Remember, the aim is to make this a lasting habit.

Tips and Notes

1. Be Genuine: Authenticity is the currency of this love bank. Write from the heart.
2. Keep It Private: This is a sacred space for both of you. Respect its privacy.
3. Revisit and Rejoice: Review previous entries and relive those moments of appreciation.

Activity: "Love Letters and Cuddles (When Words Meet Touch)"

Introduction

Ah, the lost art of love letters! In an era of emojis and text messages, taking the time to pen a heartfelt letter can be a powerful expression of love. Combine that with the simple but profoundly comforting act of cuddling, and you've got an emotional powerhouse of an evening.

Objective

Blending verbal expressions of love with physical closeness creates a multidimensional experience of intimacy.

Materials Needed

- Beautiful paper and pens
- A cozy blanket or comfortable space to cuddle
- Optional: A warm beverage to add to the coziness

Note to the Couple
This activity is like a cozy sweater for your relationship; it's comforting, warm, and nostalgic.

Detailed Steps
Step 1: Prepare Your Space
Example: Lay some cushions on the floor or set up a cozy corner with a blanket.
- Create a comfortable space where you can both write your letters and cuddle while reading them.

Step 2: Write Your Love Letters
Example: Write about the first time you knew you were in love with your partner.
- Take some time to write love letters to each other individually. Let the words flow; don't worry too much about structure or eloquence.

Step 3: Exchange and Read
Example: Sit next to each other and exchange letters.
- Once both letters are written, exchange them and read them silently or aloud to each other.

Step 4: Cuddle Time
Example: Wrap yourselves in a blanket and cuddle while discussing your favorite parts of the letters.
- After reading, move to your cuddling space and talk about the letters, sharing your favorite parts or any emotions they stirred.

Tips and Notes
1. Be Honest: Authenticity trumps poetic flair. Speak from the heart.
2. Make It a Ritual: Consider making this a monthly or yearly tradition to chronicle your love journey.
3. Keep the Letters: Store them in a special place as keepsakes of your love.

Made in the USA
Las Vegas, NV
08 January 2024

84074048R10109